Advance Praise for
Decoding Silicon Valley: The Insider's Guide

Decoding Silicon Valley

The Insider's Guide

Michelle E. Messina & Jonathan C. Baer

Decode Publishers, LLC
Redwood City, California

Printed in the United States of America.

ISBN: 978-0-9973624-0-4 (hardcover)

ISBN: 978-0-9973624-1-1 (softcover)

ISBN: 978-0-9973624-2-8 (ebook)

For more information about this book or its authors, visit www.decodingsiliconvalley.com or email authors@decodingsiliconvalley.com.

This book is available for purchase at bulk prices. Please inquire at authors@decodingsiliconvalley.com.

To my parents, Donna and David, who taught me so much, though only in hindsight have I been able to truly appreciate it; and to Claire, because you truly are a bright, clear light.

– Michelle E. Messina

To my parents, Doris and Leonard, for teaching me the value of hard work, persistence, and tenacity in the face of adversity. And to Lois, Ellie, and Alex for their love and support.

– Jonathan C. Baer

Table of Contents

Chapter 3 - The Silicon Valley You Must Experience.............................37

Understanding how to connect and build a curated network of people who can help you grow your business is as important as what actually happens in Silicon Valley. Events and meetups regularly bring people together, enabling "random, happy accidents" where people get connected. We provide some practical tips on how to pitch, we detail a number of the more common mistakes made by entrepreneurs when pitching, and we look at why pitch competitions and "demo days" are merely the first of many steps in raising capital.

Interviews:

Chapter 4 - Hidden Silicon Valley..57

The core values of Silicon Valley shape who we are, while our behavior and communication style shapes the way we do business. Many of these aspects of Valley life are not obvious, particularly if you're here only for a short time. They are hidden in plain sight, and understanding them can improve your chances of successfully mastering Silicon Valley.

Chapter 5 - The Silicon Valley Mindset 63

Silicon Valley has a unique approach to creating, growing, and scaling companies—something we call the Silicon Valley mindset. That perspective, coupled with a focus on experimentation and execution, has allowed the Valley to create large, highly profitable global businesses. Luck and serendipity can also have a significant impact on the success of startups. We look at the best practices that are used throughout the Valley, some of which can be selectively applied to startups elsewhere.

Interviews:

Chapter 6 - Breaking the Rules...and Other Tactics 91

Entrepreneurs break rules all the time—often boldly challenging conventional wisdom. In this chapter, we look at the characteristics of successful entrepreneurs and provide tips from the trenches that help you navigate the startup journey. Silicon Valley has produced both great successes and catastrophic failures. We look at a number of reasons why companies in the Valley fail.

Interviews:

Chapter 7 - Silly Valley...123

The myths and legends seem to be bigger the farther away you get from Silicon Valley. We take on twelve of the most common misconceptions that exist about Silicon Valley and set the record straight. We also include stories from Silicon Valley veterans who share some of the silly things they've seen happen in the Valley.

Interviews:

INTRODUCTION

Silicon Valley is not the birthplace of all tech-based startups, nor is it the source of all venture capital. Yet, over the past fifty years, the Valley's entrepreneurs have refined the art of company-building into a science. A certain mystique has developed about Silicon Valley, one that gets distorted and magnified the further away from the Valley you are.

After meeting thousands of entrepreneurs around the world and leading hundreds of international delegations in Silicon Valley, we know that most entrepreneurs believe Silicon Valley to be *the* place to start and build a technology company into a global institution. But how does the Valley actually work? *Decoding Silicon Valley: The Insider's Guide* is designed to help you better understand what you can see and experience here, including the more subtle aspects of the Valley, which are often hidden in plain sight. As simple as this sounds, what has surprised us is that no one has yet written a book on this topic.

We wrote the book from the perspective of the entrepreneur—the heart and soul of every startup. We designed this book to be a guide for you to use, to refer to often, and to share with your fellow entrepreneurs in your startup community. Our goal is to give you information and insight that will help you build a more successful business, wherever you are in the world.

While entrepreneurs are celebrated in Silicon Valley, elsewhere they have often been misunderstood and looked on as people who don't have a "real job." Today this attitude is changing. Entrepreneurs are everywhere—and we see an increasing acceptance of entrepreneurship as a way to develop products, build companies, create jobs, and enhance economic prosperity.

We made the assumption that most readers are like us: possessing short attention spans yet immense curiosity. We have mixed information with practical advice, and have included interviews and stories that help bring these tips to life. The chapters are written so you can read just a specific section that may interest you. The downside to this approach is that you may occasionally see some duplication where we discuss a subject in one chapter, such as product/market fit, and then expand on it in greater detail in another. So if you're someone who likes to read a book from start to finish in a single sitting, feel free to skip over those sections you find redundant.

Even though we are both veterans of numerous startups, we were surprised to discover that the effort of writing a book parallels that of building a successful startup: It's a lot harder than it looks, it takes more time than you expect, and you fail numerous times before you get it right. Whatever you write gets rewritten six, seven, or eight times. We critique entrepreneurs who believe that everyone will buy their product, and we explain how you must clearly identify those who need and want your product. We managed to forget this when we crafted the initial draft of this book, which had *something for everybody* (or so we thought). However, we took our own advice and surrounded ourselves with capable mentors and advisors who provided good advice and tough love. They told us our first draft was worse than awful. Luckily, we listened to their feedback and made our book smaller and more focused, which, ironically, created a larger potential audience. We hope it is also a better book. We learned that it took a great deal of thought and effort to get beyond the truisms, to uncover what makes Silicon Valley so unique, and to identify those factors that trip up so many entrepreneurs from outside the Valley. This book is our give-back to the global entrepreneurial community.

We have enjoyed the journey of writing this book. We hope you will enjoy reading it.

A Short History of Silicon Valley

Visiting or doing business in Silicon Valley doesn't require knowing the history of the area or how the region came to be called that name. However, understanding the decades of work that formed Silicon Valley may help you appreciate what the region is today.

Silicon Valley traces its origins back to 1909 when David Starr Jordan, the president of Stanford University, made an investment in Lee de Forest's invention of the vacuum tube. Since then, Stanford continued to encourage entrepreneurs, producing graduates such as Bill Hewlett and David Packard, who founded Hewlett-Packard, and Russell Varian, who developed the underlying technology for radar and started Varian Associates. After World War II, veterans who had served at local military bases decided to remain in the area. Many of them subsequently attended Stanford, which increased student enrollment and put financial pressure on the university. As a means of generating incremental revenue, the administration responded by establishing Stanford Industrial Park, which attracted many early tech companies and today provides office space to Silicon Valley startups and growth companies.

William Shockley, the inventor of the transistor, moved to the area in the mid-1950s. Fairchild Semiconductor was founded by a number of engineers who had worked for Shockley, and two of them, Robert Noyce and Gordon Moore, later created Intel. Following the Russians' launch of Sputnik in 1957, the U.S. Government provided significant funding to Fairchild to develop technology that was used in the U.S. satellite and space programs.

The region's growing reputation for innovation attracted talent from all over the world. And when the semiconductor industry produced computer power at a cost low enough to allow tinkerers to experiment with new technologies, the personal computer industry was born.

Apple and other computer companies were launched, along with many other companies that provided supporting hardware and manufacturing capabilities. The mouse was invented at Stanford Research Institute, using funding from NASA, the U.S. Air Force, and ARPA (Advanced Research Projects Agency), a technology that soon was followed by the ARPANET—precursor to the Internet. Many of the pioneering mouse and Internet researchers were then hired by Xerox PARC, which developed object-oriented programming, graphical user interfaces, Ethernet, Postscript, and laser printers. These people and their inventions led to the formation of 3Com and Adobe, and some of these technologies further enabled such companies as Cisco, Apple, and Microsoft. After the Internet was opened for commercial business in 1995, startups—including eBay and Amazon—were founded. Although the government was instrumental in the formation of Silicon Valley, it has played an increasingly limited role in the era of the Internet.

While venture capital has fueled growth since the Valley began, a change in pension investment rules in the late 1970s allowed venture capitalists to raise large institutional funds. Before that time, most money was raised from high-net-worth individuals.

By the late 1990s, Internet firms and software companies were flourishing—until the dot-com meltdown changed the landscape in early 2000. The wave of companies that sprang up after the bubble burst were primarily mobile, gaming, social media, and SaaS (software as a service) companies, including Zynga, Facebook, LinkedIn, Twitter, and Salesforce.com. And the most recent crop have focused on the shared-economy and data-analytics sectors; these include AirBnB, Uber, and Palantir Technologies.

The region has also fueled startups in medical devices and biotech. Genentech, a pioneer in the recombinant DNA industry, was founded by a Silicon Valley venture capitalist and a researcher from the

University of California at San Francisco (UCSF), with technology developed at both Stanford University and UCSF.

Today, Silicon Valley has expanded its geographic footprint to include San Francisco, some forty miles to the north, and beyond. The variety of technologies is also much broader, ranging from traditional hardware and software to clean tech, medical devices, biotech, and agricultural products. It is a region that continues to foster innovation and entrepreneurship, as it continually reinvents itself.

So what, exactly, does "Silicon Valley" refer to? In 1972, electronics writer Don Hoefler coined the phrase because all the startups at the time were based on semiconductors, which used silicon chips; the name stuck.

PARC, a Xerox Company, in Palo Alto

CHAPTER 1
SILICON VALLEY MATTERS

It's 4:33 a.m. and you can hear the early-morning call to prayer in Cairo, Egypt. The city is bathed in fog and darkness, and the city's roads are unusually quiet.

Only the day before, while sitting in traffic, we realized that there are no traffic lights, no stop signs, and no posted speed limits in Cairo. When you can see painted lane stripes on the roads, they are completely ignored. A three-lane road becomes four and sometimes five lanes as every driver inches forward, competing for an ever-better position. The car to the left of us is close enough to smell, with just inches between our door and theirs. The windows are open, music is blaring, and we seem to be smoking the other driver's cigarette.

The streets are dusty and dirty—full of potholes, stalled cars, and speed bumps that make thoroughfares more like slalom courses. Egyptian cars, for the most part, suffer through this contact sport. They are dented and scratched, and held together with the likes of clear tape, wire, rope, and fabric. Driving in Cairo is a strategic undertaking, a chess game requiring quick reflexes to avoid the pothole in the road, to slip into an opening in the traffic flow, or simply to move forward.

The ability of Egyptian drivers to make it across town, or across the country, speaks volumes about their strong spirit and tenacity, and is representative of the entrepreneurial spirit we encounter in emerging and transitional economies all over the world.

After working in dozens of countries, and crisscrossing the globe on both United and American Airlines for many years, it has become abundantly clear to us that entrepreneurs are the heart and soul of economic growth and diversity, and the primary job creators throughout the world. They function as the essential connective tissue between countries and among people in today's global economy. Governments may fall, industries may collapse, and politicians' priorities may change. Yet entrepreneurs remain—jumping in amid tremendous uncertainty, adapting as necessary, and finding opportunities as borders and markets change.

But what does it take for these entrepreneurs to be successful? The environment plays a key role in facilitating what is otherwise the difficult and convoluted process of turning an idea into a business, creating something from nothing, or spinning straw into gold.

The Silicon Valley Ecosystem

Having worked in many regions of the United States and around the world, we are acutely aware that not all entrepreneurs have a supportive ecosystem in which to build their companies. That's why in this book we hope to decode for you Silicon Valley's unique ecosystem and describe the business practices that Valley startups employ to identify market opportunities, build better products, and scale more quickly in the pursuit of global businesses. Doing so can reveal a great deal about resilience, risk, failure, uncertainty, the pioneering spirit, and the boom-and-bust cycles of business here—all the while deepening your understanding of the best practices for sustaining vibrant business environments organized for the benefit of entrepreneurs and startups everywhere.

> ❝ *If you cannot be the best in the world, do something else.* ❞
>
> — Joe Kennedy, Pandora

People come from all over the world to visit Silicon Valley. Some just want a photograph in front of Facebook, a meal at the famous Google cafeteria, or a chance to see the offices of 500 Startups. Others arrive ready to pitch their ideas to a prominent venture capitalist on Sand Hill Road, or to seek a meeting with the CEO of Cisco. Yet for savvy entrepreneurs, economic development agencies, and policy makers alike around the world, Silicon Valley offers far more: It offers a chance to see a highly functioning ecosystem that supports and nurtures startups like nowhere else.

> *Silicon Valley is special because of the ecosystem where everyone is doing the same stuff. It's easy to talk about any aspect of tech, and it's always possible to get help from someone.*
>
> — David Lee, SK Telecom

There are those who try to duplicate the Valley elsewhere by implementing a few startup pitch competitions, a demo day, a government venture capital program, some random classes and workshops, and an educational trip to Silicon Valley itself. But ecosystems are far more complex than that: they are made up of people, cultures, ideas, attitudes, perceptions, and, in some cases, myths and legends. It takes a great deal of time and tremendous patience for an ecosystem to mature and work efficiently. And Silicon Valley has had a decades-long head start over the rest of the world.

"Silicon Valley is like an algorithm." – Martin Pichinson

Martin Pichinson

Martin Pichinson is the CEO of agencyIP, a company that licenses technology for both large and small companies. He is also the founder and co-CEO of Sherwood Partners, a leading firm that handles the shutdown of failed venture-backed companies.

"Silicon Valley is like an algorithm that works. There are really smart people here, there is money available from investors, there is infrastructure, and there is a desire to create change. There is also a strong support system of mentors and others working together to make it all happen. Simply put...everything you need to win is here in Silicon Valley. Others claim, 'We are going to be the next Silicon Valley,' but history tells us this usually does not happen. Is there another Wall Street? Another Hollywood? No. Some people say that Seattle is a hotbed of startups because of Microsoft, or Austin, Texas, because of Dell. But most major trends and players come out of Silicon Valley, which only reinforces the concept that the algorithm is here. Without total alignment, the Silicon Valley algorithm would not work, but since things are all in place, everything works together to create greatness.

"Silicon Valley is just like Hollywood or Wall Street. None of these regions were planned; they just happened organically, developing what was necessary in order to be successful. If you're filming a movie in Hollywood and the camera breaks, there are organizations that can supply a new camera immediately. Same thing happens in Silicon Valley. If the CEO of a company is terminated or quits, a board can find a new interim CEO quickly. For years, people have been saying that Hollywood is going to disappear since it's cheaper to make films elsewhere. But the reality is that people continue to make movies in Hollywood because the infrastructure and the tools are there. The same thing applies in Silicon Valley. It would be hard to grow Silicon Valley elsewhere."

The Mystique and the Truth

Movies, the press, and entrepreneurs themselves have all contributed to the perception that Silicon Valley is the only place to start and build a successful company. Many people believe that just *being in Silicon Valley* will make them successful. Silicon Valley is viewed as the epicenter of the tech startup world—the place where you will find everything you need to start and grow your company. This is what we call the *Silicon Valley mystique.*

As a result of this mystique, entrepreneurs flock to the region to build their global companies, change the world, or get wealthy. They also come here to raise capital, find customers, and develop partnerships. The sheer number of large, successful companies reinforces the mystique. Apple, eBay, Google, Facebook, Intel, Cisco, Saleforce.com, Uber, AirBnB, PayPal—these companies all have become household brands, familiar to consumers and business people around the world. And they all were founded in Silicon Valley, or moved to the region early in their history.

> " *Anybody can make their dreams come true in Silicon Valley.* "
>
> —Kayvan Baroumand, SV101 Ventures

How much of this mystique is true? Let us begin to answer that question by providing you with a few statistics and facts about the Valley and its surroundings:

- $94 billion in venture capital is under management in California today.

- Silicon Valley companies are among the most active acquirers of startups worldwide: in 2014, Apple, Oracle, Facebook, Yahoo, and Google alone bought a total of 77 companies.

- The market valuation of private companies in Silicon Valley is often 2 to 10 times that of companies located elsewhere.

- A significant number of the best, brightest, and most ambitious individuals come here to start companies or join startups. Being an entrepreneur in the Valley is considered cool, not just something you do if you can't get a real job.

- This is a place where a lot of new ideas are developed, refined, and transformed into viable businesses. There is a willingness to entertain big ideas that, at first glance, seem impossible; at second glance, infeasible; and at third glance, impractical.

- There's a unique cadre of experienced and knowledgeable people in Silicon Valley who have broad business and technical expertise, and who are capable of transforming ideas into viable businesses.

- Investors in Silicon Valley are willing to bet on smart people and great ideas long before startups show significant business traction.

- Investors who are well connected to customers in the Valley (what is typically referred to as "smart money") often do help startups. There are customers here who will take a chance on a startup by buying product, providing feedback, and serving as a reference customer for that startup.

- Events, conferences, and networks here provide an unprecedented level of visibility, enabling startups to gain a 360° view of the market, the competition, and customer trends.

- The number and diversity of large corporations located in Silicon Valley provide startups with access to a range of potential partnership opportunities and acquirers.

- It is easier to build a global business here than anywhere else.

- While you cannot meet everybody, you can meet almost anyone here.

"The Valley sets a high bar for startups everywhere in the world.... This drives entrepreneurs elsewhere to be better." – Chris Shipley

Chris Shipley

Chris Shipley is a journalist, technology analyst, and former executive producer of the DEMO conference. She has worked with startups all over the world.

"There are numerous misconceptions about Silicon Valley. Those outside the region, and even some locals, think of the Valley as a company-building place. But it's really more of a capital-building place. Entrepreneurs in Boston create groundbreaking products that can change how things work in the world. They are building companies that will have an impact on the world. By contrast, if you ask the typical entrepreneur in Silicon Valley why he is doing what he is doing, he'll tell you it is to make money. Silicon Valley is about wealth and wealth creation—a very different perspective from what you find in startup communities in Boston, Gdansk, or Athens.

"Another misconception that many outsiders have about the Valley: You pitch, you get the attention of someone world famous, you raise capital, and you're all set. It's easy! But those same people fail to realize how incredibility competitive it is. They spend a lot of time going to events, meetups, and conferences—and they fail to realize that they also have to do real work. It's not just about the hustle.

"Does Silicon Valley matter in the grand scheme of things? Yes, in an aspirational sense. The Valley sets a high bar for startups everywhere in the world. If you can make it in the Valley, you can make it anywhere. Regardless of whether it's true or not, this idea drives entrepreneurs elsewhere to be better."

> *When you first come here, you're in awe—sometimes too much so. But after a while you acclimate. You say to yourself, 'They're good, but they're just like me,' or 'I'm just like them.' Then you really can step up your game.*

— Dave McClure, 500 Startups

Little Lies

You'll hear lots of things about the Valley that turn out to be simply untrue. While we don't want to discourage you from visiting or starting your company here, you should be aware of these little lies:

- **"Silicon Valley is the only place to build a global tech company."** Many large, successful tech companies have been created and grown in other regions of the world. Here are some examples: Tencent is a large Chinese portal and gaming company; Alibaba, another Chinese company, is one the world's largest ecommerce companies; and Mercado Libre is Latin America's largest ecommerce company.

- **"All good innovation comes from Silicon Valley."** Bright entrepreneurs are everywhere. By our last count, we've worked with entrepreneurs from over 50 countries who are successfully building local, regional, and global businesses.

- **"We take risks because it's okay to fail."** We do take risks, but we don't fixate on failure. We fixate on success. If you're always worried about failing, you limit your opportunities to be successful.

- **"In Silicon Valley, unlimited money is available, and it's easy to raise capital."** While it's easier to raise capital in the Valley than elsewhere, it's still hard. Competition to secure venture financing is very intense because investors are focused on investing in the best products and the best teams.

- **"In a few short years, you can easily build a $1B company and sell it!"** Most Silicon Valley companies take a minimum of four years—and more likely seven to ten years—to reach the point of acquisition or IPO (initial public offering). Exceptions occur, but they're rare. It's a long, slow process.

- **"Everyone is waiting for you to show up."** There are tens of thousands of startups in Silicon Valley, plus thousands more entrepreneurs from outside the region who visit here each year. In this fast-paced, dynamic environment full of competitors and deal flow, no one is sitting around waiting for you. The companies that succeed here are ambitious, thoughtful, and extremely good at getting sh*t done.

> ❝ *There is a misconception that if you just show up, the magic will happen. It is all easy only in hindsight when the story is glorified.* ❞
>
> — Chris Shipley, Journalist and Tech Analyst

- **"There is a secret handshake, or code word, that will make you an insider—and ensure your success."** Nope, there isn't. Some companies succeed on the basis of sheer luck and timing. Others fail for precisely the same reasons. Being well connected provides an advantage in building your business, but even companies with great teams and top-tier investors can fail, and do.

- **"There is something in the air or water in the Valley—a special, magic fairy dust."** Of course not. We think this myth stems from the fact that Silicon Valley has refined a formula for creating startups that is based on learning by doing, bringing in people who have done it before, and having all the critical resources centralized in one place.

"As soon as entrepreneurs come here, they either get meetings or they don't" – Mark White

Mark White

Mark White is a partner in the Silicon Valley law firm of White Summers Caffee & James.

Mark White has worked with hundreds of international founders from all over the world who come to Silicon Valley seeking the 3 C's: customers, capital, and connections. These entrepreneurs learn very quickly whether their ventures will succeed.

"As an entrepreneur, you come here to find out what you know and what you don't know. You want to find out if you can beat other people to market. Or if you're doing the wrong thing. And it's what you don't know that you're more afraid of. That's because you can control what you know. The pace in Silicon Valley is driven a lot by fear.

"In Silicon Valley, you find out right away if you have a viable venture. As soon as entrepreneurs come here, either they get meetings or they don't. They get immediate feedback in an evening: You're crazy or you're not. It's a great proving ground for new business concepts, new business models, and new products. And while the information is always imperfect, it's better here than anywhere else."

The mystique of Silicon Valley has helped to attract many smart people from all over the world, and these people have built large successful companies—which makes Silicon Valley, in many ways, a self-fulfilling prophecy. However, we don't buy into the idea that Silicon Valley is the only place to build companies. Many large, successful, tech-based companies have been started and scaled elsewhere. Further, we see business ecosystems quickly changing in other regions of the world. We see smart, driven, and resourceful entrepreneurs with great ideas who have figured out how to get traction in their local markets and raise capital. We also see serial entrepreneurs who have gained deep insight from their past successes and failures and who are more likely to be successful the next time around. And we see investors developing deeper understanding of the startup journey and how they can add value.

> ❝ *Silicon Valley is egalitarian. Talent rules.* ❞
>
> — Selcuk Atli, Serial Entrepreneur

The Silicon Valley Mindset

Silicon Valley has a mindset that leads to a disciplined approach to building global-scale businesses. While this approach is not a rigid formula, we know from experience that most successful Silicon Valley companies sooner or later do follow it.

So what is the Silicon Valley mindset behind this approach? It is composed of four elements:

- How we look at businesses
- How we identify market opportunities
- How we identify the best customers to target
- How we scale small businesses into global companies

If you come to Silicon Valley, your ideas will be evaluated on the basis of these criteria, as are those of every entrepreneur—at least initially.

> *" The experience of being in Silicon Valley, and competing with lots of really talented people, raises your game. "*
>
> — Dave McClure, 500 Startups

Mystique can be a powerful magnet, and Silicon Valley's mystique is legendary. The Valley has the right elements, attitudes, and resources in place to enable entrepreneurs to build something significant from nothing. In the next chapters, we decode more of the elements of Silicon Valley that support entrepreneurs in building global companies. So stay with us.

CHAPTER 2
The Silicon Valley You Can See

Turkish-born serial entrepreneur Selcuk Atli knew he had to be in Silicon Valley. "Everybody who has made it comes out of Silicon Valley," he will tell you. "If you want to go into finance, you go to New York City. If you want to build a company, you go to Silicon Valley."

Silicon Valley has that reputation. "Rags to riches" stories are legendary in which companies are sold for millions—or even billions—all in just a few short years.

Is this the way the Valley works? Will you make billions here? It's possible, but not probable. Most companies do not achieve a billion-dollar valuation—or if they do, it's certainly not in the course of a few years. But many companies *are* successful in Silicon Valley, where success is measured in millions, tens of millions, or even hundreds of millions. And your company could be one of those, though it may take five to seven years. Starting a company in Silicon Valley is not dissimilar to going to Las Vegas or Macao for a weekend at the tables; it's a gamble, and the probability of hitting the jackpot is low.

As we travel the world, we're often asked questions about Silicon Valley. Some of the more common ones are: *Where is it? Does it have a fence around it? Who runs the place?* If you haven't visited, it's difficult to understand what makes the Valley unique. But once you're here, many of the ecosystem's parts are plain to see—and worthy of study. What makes Silicon Valley function so well is that we have an ecosystem made up of super-smart people and supportive institutions.

> *Though individual venture investors are not always right, Silicon Valley, as a whole, is more right than wrong. The collaborative ecosystem does a pretty good job of picking winning new products. And it is constantly reinventing itself by scouring the world for the best and the brightest.*
>
> — John Scull, Southern Cross Venture Partners

Let's deconstruct this ecosystem and take a close look at its components. Love it, hate it, or try to imitate it—Silicon Valley has been an engine of innovation for the past fifty-plus years.

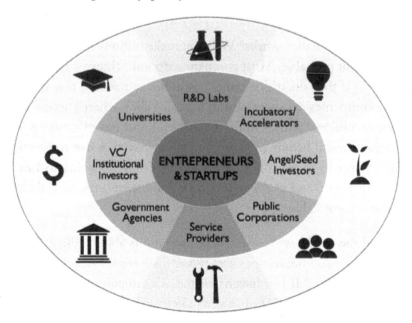

Silicon Valley ecosystem

Entrepreneurs

By far the most important people of the Valley are entrepreneurs. While some start companies in order to make millions, many more are driven by the desire to make a difference. They are passionate, creative, and driven to succeed. They're also very bright and sometimes willing to take risks that look irrational or foolish to others. Without these innovators, there would be no startups.

> *I want to create things and move the universe in ways I think the universe should be moved. If that means starting a company, then I'll do that. I don't think you have to be an entrepreneur to have this kind of impact, but I don't have talent in any other area, so the path for me is entrepreneurship.*
>
> — Phil Libin, Evernote
> and General Catalyst Partners

We're fortunate to have lots of entrepreneurs in the Valley. Some have grown up in Palo Alto or San Francisco or other areas in Northern California—but most are from other parts of the world, sometimes from as far away as Uzbekistan or Estonia or India. Some leave big companies such as Microsoft or Google to start their own companies. Some work for a time at others' startups, both successful and unsuccessful, before launching their own ventures. Some hold down day jobs, at Stanford Medical Center, for example, while they work on developing something new (such as groundbreaking medical technologies) in their spare time. Entrepreneurs in the Valley come from a broad range of industries; and most have either technical or sales and marketing backgrounds. The average age of a Silicon Valley entrepreneur is 38, certainly older than the stereotype, and most are male.

> ❝ *The great entrepreneur–leader needs both chutzpah and humility.* ❞
>
> — Joe Kennedy, Pandora

Good entrepreneurs are smart, passionate, and a little crazy. They are also confident, almost to the point of arrogance. Yet the good ones are also coachable, and not delusional. The smart ones work with mentors who make sure they have access to different perspectives. But a CEO's job to is to make decisions and live with them. After all, it's their company.

"Don't be greedy" – Selcuk Atli

Selcuk Atli

Selcuk Atli is cofounder of SocialWire, Boostable, and Nomadic Mentors. He is also an Entrepreneur-in-Residence (EIR) at 500 Startups.

"Don't be greedy," Selcuk Atli advises on the topic of raising money. "Raising less money at a lower price from better investors is far better than raising more money at a higher valuation from those who cannot help you or your company. Good investors are worth far more than just the money they provide. They are plugged into Silicon Valley. You still have to do 99 percent of the work yourself—but raising money from smart, well-connected investors is a signal that you are doing something important. Could I have gotten those meetings, those hires, those customers, those partners without those people? Perhaps. But surrounding yourself with the right people makes the job easier.

"The challenge for startups is that it's really hard to know what a customer wants unless you show them something first. So you need vaporware— something you can show either to get a commitment to buy or to find out what the customer really wants. You can lead the customer to believe that you are a lot further along in producing the product than you really are, but you can't lie. This is a typical way to test a b-to-b product. For a b-to-c product, put up a Facebook page and take credit cards. Fulfill orders manually, if necessary. This is a good way to see if anyone wants your product before spending money to build out a fully functional version."

Customers

One of the virtues of Silicon Valley is the high concentration of potential customers—big and small, hi-tech and low—within an hour's drive. This allows a startup to work in close proximity to its target market, which is important for multiple reasons. First, customer proximity allows a startup team to hone its concept and validate its product in the marketplace: does the product fit the customer's environment and solve the customer's problem? Second, customer proximity helps the startup team drive future product functionality and fine-tune its product roadmap. Third, it affords the startup team the opportunity to develop relationships that can lead to customer references and referrals—important ways that startups secure follow-on customers. And finally, customer proximity is useful when a problem arises: Startups that are able to quickly address what's not working build trust and customer retention.

Feedback provided by initial customers often leads to refinements in a startup's product. But sometimes it reveals that a startup has gotten the product completely wrong. In such cases, a startup will often "pivot"—a buzzword in Silicon Valley used to describe companies that completely change their product or customer focus, or both. One example of a successful "pivot" of a business-to-consumer company is Yelp, a company that has set the standard for reviews of restaurants, retailers, and services. Yelp was initially a site for rating one's experience on a date.

Business customers in the Valley are willing to risk buying products from unproven startups when the founders, management team, or investors are known to those customers. Such personal relationships are how many effective startups find early customers and gain market traction.

" In digital software, specialization of the product really matters. Increasingly, customers are doing their own research since so much information is changing. Therefore sales and marketing are fundamentally changing. In the past people had to sell it; now early customers get all the information and they make their own decisions. Early adopters are looking for new things—if it is a great product, then they're willing to trial it. They don't want to be sold, they do the work themselves. "

— John Scull, Southern Cross Venture Partners

Government

Many businesspeople working abroad think there must be a central governmental agency behind the well-oiled machine that is Silicon Valley. We're often asked: *Who starts and stops it? Who greases the gears? Who checks the speed and adjusts the knobs?* These questions arise in part because so many economies around the world are planned, regulated, and kept in sync by one or more government entities.

In fact, the Silicon Valley ecosystem today enjoys essentially no government intervention. For many visitors, this is a strange and difficult idea to comprehend. Regional development in the Valley, when it does occur, is typically business-led rather than government-led. And among the many companies here, what little government exists is largely irrelevant when it comes to the technologies that get developed and the markets that are addressed.

In the early days of Silicon Valley, the U.S. federal government was the primary source of funding for much of the basic research performed at large corporations and universities here. Through military and aerospace contracts, the government was responsible for the development of the early hardware systems, semiconductor chips, and other silicon-based products that helped give the Valley its name; and numerous startups were formed to commercialize and market the resulting products. But today, government funding produces only a minor part of the research useful to startups in Silicon Valley. Nor does the U.S. Government play a role in determining the areas of focus for most startups, as do governments in numerous other countries. By contrast, market forces here determine which technologies are commercialized, which companies get funded, and ultimately which companies succeed or fail.

However, the government does play an important role in enabling innovation to occur—though it is a role national in scope that covers all fifty states, not just Silicon Valley. Specifically, the government provides a legal framework that makes it easy to set up a new business. A new company can become a legal entity literally within hours. Winding it down can take longer, but dissolution is measured in weeks or months, not years or decades. Moreover, when companies fail, founders and investors are not held financially responsible for company liabilities. The US has a strong tort system for enforcing contracts, as well as clear laws that protect patents and other intellectual property. And at the federal, state, and local levels, there are no undue bureaucratic requirements, no unwieldy permits, and no overly burdensome taxes or fees that hinder startup formation and growth.

The government agencies that *do* exist in Silicon Valley are primarily offices of economic development established by other countries to provide landing spots for startups based in their own regions. These countries read like a list from the United Nations: Brazil, Korea, Denmark, Norway, Germany, Estonia, Canada, the United Kingdom, Mexico, Northern Ireland, and Poland. And that's only a partial list.

Universities

If innovation, planning, and direction aren't coming from the government, then they must be coming from the Valley's institutions of learning—Stanford, UC Berkeley, UC San Francisco, San Jose State University, and other local universities, right?

It's true that Sergey Brin and Larry Page were graduate students at Stanford when they started Google, and that Jerry Yang founded Yahoo while a student at Stanford. However, neither Google nor Yahoo was the result of a university research initiative. Both were projects initiated by those graduate students themselves.

Peter Marcotullio of SRI International, the contract research lab spun out of Stanford after World War II, explains: "At Stanford and at most research universities, there is no planned, top-down research or commercialization agenda. What they have is a competitive academic culture, access to world-class investors and entrepreneurs, and established mechanisms to transition from lab to market. Successful startups don't necessarily come straight from research into the market. They need to identify and address a need. The Stanford Graduate School of Business offers several programs on entrepreneurship that encourage business students to team with engineering students to integrate technology and market innovations."

Intellectual property (IP) developed specifically by Stanford goes through its Office of Technology Licensing. However, not all Stanford-incubated startups are based on Stanford-generated IP. The school's Ignite program and its Center for Entrepreneurial Studies both generate many startup ideas, as does the multidisciplinary design program known as the d.school. Stanford also has a student-run incubation program, called StartX, which provides Stanford-affiliated entrepreneurs with mentors, office space, and other help in building their businesses.

Stanford and the other universities in the Valley foster an environment that allows people to take innovative technologies and create new businesses. Also, the universities are magnets for smart people. Each academic year, a new crop of students and faculty members migrates to the Valley from every corner of the world. Many stay—attracted by the energy, lifestyle, culture, and weather here, along with the opportunities to create their own companies in the epicenter of the startup world.

Stanford University Campus

Government and Corporate Research Labs

Transistors, the computer mouse, and more recent innovations have come from work done in government and corporate research labs. SRI International probably enjoys the best track record for spinning out core innovations into separate companies, some of which have become very successful businesses. Among its innovations, SRI is responsible for Nuance, a speech recognition company; Siri, the voice in your iPhone; and certain advanced CT scan technologies jointly developed with Stanford University and now licensed to General Electric and Siemens. SRI has also developed technologies for robotic navigation which has been widely licensed, and software-based image stabilization licensed to Google for the Android phones. Other laboratories, including PARC (a subsidiary of Xerox) and Livermore National Laboratories, also engage in leading-edge research that attracts top technical talent from around the world.

> *"The professionalization of the angel community is all new in the last five years."* – Ann Winblad

Ann Winblad

Ann Winblad is a cofounder and managing general partner at Hummer Winblad Venture Partners, a pioneering venture capital firm founded in 1989. She was also the cofounder and CEO of Open Source, a company that was sold for $15 million in 1984.

"When I first got into the venture business, there were no professional angel networks. The people who invested in startups were a dinner club of old people with extra money. In most cases, they didn't add a lot of value.

"That scenario has changed significantly. The growth in angel funding has allowed more money to go into companies. Today there exists a great variety of angel investors—including many women. Broadway Angels is a Silicon Valley group that includes a broad range of entrepreneurs, technology executives, and semi-retired venture capitalists who are funding women entrepreneurs.

"The standard pitch to angel investors is one about a product—a smart dog dish, for example. This is a very different pitch from one you might present to VCs [venture capitalists]. As VCs, we cannot fund smart dog dishes. We need to fund pet companies.

"If you just want to build a product, consider creating a crowdsource campaign. To do this, you have to learn how to build a great video and use social media. There are many examples of startups funded through this kind of angel approach. Oculus was funded first through Kickstarter; it later raised venture capital funding before being acquired by Facebook. But not everyone is successful in crowdfunding. You need to be mindful of the audience, the process, the social support, and what your 'giveback' is."

"Today angel and seed investing is multiplying because those who have earned wealth from successful exits feel obligated to reinvest it. A group of WhatsApp employees met with me after their company was acquired by Facebook. They wanted to know how much of their newfound wealth should be set aside to fund other entrepreneurs. They felt that it was a real gift to have made it big-time, and they wanted to help other entrepreneurs going forward."

"The US JOBS Act allows companies to raise money from many individuals as well as from platforms such as Kickstarter and AngelList. The professionalization of the angel community is all-new in the last five years."

"But the venture capital business itself hasn't changed. The number of Series A rounds is still relatively small, though the quality of the companies that VCs have the opportunity to fund has improved. We love to see angel-funded companies. With a little angel money an entrepreneur can show a lot to A-round investors. Although Hyperion was launched in 1995 by two guys with a PowerPoint presentation and ultimately sold to Oracle for about $3 billion, we no longer have to make our decisions on the basis of two guys and a PowerPoint presentation."

Investors

In Silicon Valley investors play an important role. They have funded thousands of well-known companies, including Google, Facebook, and Uber.

Investors come in three flavors. Perhaps the most well-known are those in the traditional venture capital firms, such as Sequoia Capital, Benchmark Capital, Kleiner Perkins, and Andreessen Horowitz. Venture capitalists in these firms are full-time investors who manage funds that consist of pension monies, endowments, and investments from high-net-worth individuals. They often focus their investments on certain sectors of technology, or on companies at certain stages of growth.

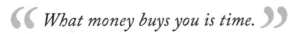

What money buys you is time.

— David Lee, SK Telecom

The second category consists of angel investors, who invest their own money. Frequently they belong to a group with a structured approach to screening and evaluating deals, but the decision to invest is an individual one. Angel investors typically invest in early-stage companies that align with their individual investment criteria and areas of interest. Many, if not most, of the VCs and angel investors in the Valley have served in senior management roles at startups, or have started one or more companies themselves.

Google campus in Mountain View

Finally, there are corporate investors who invest for strategic reasons—frequently to gain an early look at emerging technologies and startups. Sometimes their interest leads to selective acquisitions. Corporate venture capital has grown considerably over the past decade. In 2015, some 30 percent of all venture financing included one or more corporate investors.

While the funding that investors provide is important to startups, the advice and contacts they can offer are of even greater value. Typically, advice centers on recruiting, troubleshooting, dealing with customers, and overcoming go-to-market challenges. Larger venture firms often have teams that assist entrepreneurs with recruitment, operational issues, social media, and marketing efforts. And sometimes these VCs introduce entrepreneurs to senior executives running large, public companies—people in whom the VC may have invested in the past. These introductions can result in customer relationships, partnerships, and even acquisitions.

Crowdfunding

While crowdfunding is important in Silicon Valley, it plays a much less important role than angel, seed, or venture capital funding. Most crowdfunding platforms, including Kickstarter and Indiegogo, are used to fund *products*, not companies. Typically, the money raised represents an advance purchase of the product. While a number of differences exist among platforms, the biggest is that some, such as Kickstarter, require that a company be incorporated in the United States, while others, such as Indiegogo, do not.

Kickstarter is perhaps the most well known of the crowdsourcing platforms. It has hosted over 250,000 campaigns, of which about a third have been successful. The most successful funded projects on Kickstarter have been in the music and video areas. Other notable campaigns include the Pebble Smartwatch, which raised over $10 million, and the Coolest Cooler, which raised over $13 million.

Several platforms now enable entrepreneurs to raise funds and simultaneously grow their businesses through equity crowdfunding. In this type of funding, equity in the company is sold for cash. These platforms include The Fundable and Angelist, the latter for qualified investors only. The U.S. Government recently passed legislation to lessen the regulatory burdens on small businesses and legalize equity crowdfunding by individuals.

Particularly for startups with hardware products, crowdfunding can serve as a way to validate the market and get the company to a point where a round of venture funding is feasible. This strategy was successfully employed by Fitbit, which went public in 2015 with a valuation of over $4 billion.

The skills required to raise money through a crowdsource platform are different from those required to build either a product or a large company. Many successful crowdsource campaigns have used social media to spread the word about their projects ahead of listing them on a crowdsource site. In some instances a crowdsource campaign has become too successful—and a startup has had difficulty meeting promised product delivery schedules. This happened to Pebble, Galileo, and Oculus Rift, among many others. Nonetheless, for entrepreneurs who want to raise money and build consumer awareness, crowdsourcing can be an attractive option.

CB Insights recently reported that $321 million in venture capital financing was invested in hardware startups that had previously crowdfunded projects through Kickstarter and Indiegogo. And of those companies, 9.5 percent went on to raise venture capital financing. Notably, CB Insights saw no relationship between the amount of money raised in a crowdfunding campaign and the money subsequently raised from venture investors.

Service Professionals

Silicon Valley has one of the largest and best-developed networks of service professionals in the world. Professional services—legal, tax, accounting, payroll, PR, product testing, marketing, and more—are easily accessible and can be quite cost-effective for startups. There's no need to initially hire a full-time bookkeeper, accountant, or CFO. Silicon Valley offers nearly every service *à la carte*. Each of the major national accounting firms, including PriceWaterhouseCoopers (PWC), KPMG, Ernst & Young, and Deloitte, has practice areas devoted to working with startup companies.

Attorneys are particularly valuable resources for startup companies, offering legal services and valuable business advice. What's more, many attorneys will help startups long before they have the money to pay for legal services. These attorneys become de facto seed investors, deferring a portion of their fees until the startup raises outside capital. However, the reality is that many attorneys are selective and will only take on clients who they believe have a good chance of being successful. We have a saying: "Hire the best attorneys you cannot afford; because you can afford them."

> *There are sophisticated, global resources here in Silicon Valley. I believe companies should start their international expansion from here because they can access any market in the world. The linkages are all here.*
>
> — Kayvan Baroumand, SV101 Ventures

Attorneys also play an important role in connecting entrepreneurs to potential team members and investors, often hosting events at law offices that draw together clients with others in the ecosystem. Silicon Valley has a number of firms that have grown up with the tech industry, including Wilson Sonsini, DLA Piper, Perkins Coie, White Summers, and Fenwick & West. These firms have extensive experience representing startup companies as well as venture investors in financial transactions.

Several years ago we were asked by a well-known research firm to help spearhead an initiative to drive entrepreneurial growth in Florida. Over a number of months, we met many local lawyers—most of whom would hand us a business card and offer to provide legal work. One day we were introduced to a lawyer who worked for a major Silicon Valley law firm with an office in Atlanta. The lawyer handed us his card and offered to introduce us to investors, entrepreneurs, and other well-connected people in the southeast U.S. This lawyer clearly understood that providing introductions was an integral part of his job. He was the one we called when the time was right.

While this isn't what most lawyers do elsewhere, in Silicon Valley it is the norm.

Financial Institutions

Silicon Valley has a range of financial institutions that serve and support the startup ecosystem. These include banks, such as Silicon Valley Bank and Bridge Bank, which focus on providing services to both startups and more mature venture-backed companies. Venture leasing firms provide equipment leases, while venture debt firms specialize in providing loans to startups. What is unique about these financial institutions is their willingness to provide services to companies whose balance sheet and income statements would not support traditional banking criteria. In Silicon Valley the banks look at the track record of the CEO, the business potential of the startup, and the quality of the venture investors as part of their decision-making process. All the major investment banking firms have satellite operations in Silicon Valley to support companies looking to go public, or to provide merger-and-acquisition assistance to larger companies seeking to buy startups.

Incubators, Accelerators, and Co-working Spaces

Silicon Valley is home to hundreds of incubators, accelerators and co-working spaces. Some of the incubators and accelerators are sector-specific—focusing on digital products, hardware, wearables, educational technology, and so forth—while others are more general. Despite the fact that the terms are often used interchangeably, *incubators* are generally designed for businesses in the early concept phase, while *accelerators* are focused on helping companies gain market traction and better product-market fit. The better-known incubators, such as TechStars, Y Combinator, and 500Startups, are highly selective about whom they accept into their programs.

"Not all incubators are created equal."

— Andy Tsao, Silicon Valley Bank

Andy Tsao

Andy Tsao is a managing director of Silicon Valley Bank and leads its Global Gateway, which assists innovation companies in emerging markets with their U.S. and international expansion.

"All the incubators in the Valley ask entrepreneurs for about the same amount of equity," Andy Tsao observes, "but not all incubators are created equal. A few do a consistently good job—Y Combinator and Tech Stars, for example." Tsao believes that getting into Y Combinator is worth the price of relocating to the Valley. And he has heard from his peers that 500 Startups is more valuable for an entrepreneur than going to business school. "There are real benefits for entrepreneurs who work around one another, taking notes and collaborating. On the other hand, relocating just to get into an incubator may not make as much sense as finding a local one."

Co-working spaces, such as Galvanize and RocketSpace, have less-stringent criteria. They offer shared office space for rent by the hour, the day, or month, but they lack hands-on mentoring. Some co-working spaces also house incubators or accelerators. One example of these is GSVlabs, which operates multiple vertically focused accelerators.

Many incubators and accelerators provide access to networks of mentors and advisors who can provide advice and guidance; and some sector-specific incubators offer connections to mentors with particularly deep vertical expertise. Highly tailored programs that vary in length from weeks to months are also common. Many incubators and accelerators also offer small amounts of capital, often in the form of bridge loans, which are later converted to equity. The better-known incubators and accelerators, particularly those with successful track records, provide their companies with good access to angel and venture capital investors, both on an ad hoc basis and on "demo days." Since incubators, accelerators, and co-working spaces vary widely in terms of the content and lengths of their programs, entrepreneurs need to make sure there is a good match between the offerings and their own needs.

> *The value of accelerators has been diluted over time. More and more people have taken advantage of them, jumping between different ones just to get money.*
>
> — David Lee, SK Telecom

For most startup teams, joining a community of entrepreneurs can be far more attractive than locating office space, finding mentors, and piecing together other necessary resources on their own. Members of these communities support and learn from one another—a benefit we think is incredibly valuable. We believe that a significant part of the value beyond the contacts, the capital, and the learning is having an appreciation of how Silicon Valley works. This vantage point is what we call the *Silicon Valley perspective*. One of the primary reasons that many companies want to spend time in Silicon Valley is to gain this perspective.

Is there some secret sauce to incubators and accelerators? Perhaps. Being a graduate of a well-known incubator or accelerator brings a cachet that can be helpful in raising capital and gaining market traction. It's common knowledge that smart entrepreneurs who get the right help have a much higher chance of being successful.

"The goal of accelerators is very different from that of investors, but they both want some kind of return on investment in the end." – David Lee

David Lee

David Lee is a venture partner at SK Telecom and a cofounder of Kstartup, an early-stage accelerator located in Seoul, Korea. He is also a limited partner in both Y Combinator and Silicon Valley Angels

"Some people go in [to an accelerator] hoping to be coached. They know that they don't know everything. Others just want money. They take advantage of the system, just going to the meetings and to office hours. And that's okay, because if they come out with a great company, that's how they did it. But people running accelerators want entrepreneurs who are looking to be educated and who want to participate. Mentors will always meet entrepreneurs with the right mindset, because these entrepreneurs are coachable. And entrepreneurs who are open-minded benefit from these mentors."

Mentors, Coaches, and Advisors

Silicon Valley is home to many people who regularly mentor and advise startups. A number of them are associated with accelerators and incubators. Others, including executives at Silicon Valley companies, are willing to provide mentoring help to a startup company if the startup is of interest to them. Some angel investors are also mentors. All these mentors can provide great value and perspective because they have worked with a number of startups. They bring experience, objectivity, and—often—new contacts and valuable insights.

What's the difference between a mentor, a coach, and an advisor? A mentor provides a startup with overall business advice and guidance and may help with specific tasks such as validating the market or helping to craft the presentation or pitch deck. Typically, mentors are brought in for short-term engagements.

A coach trains the entrepreneur in a specific task, or offers a specific set of skills, such as pitch coaching.

An advisor is engaged in a more formal, longer-term relationship. Many companies also have advisory boards that may be business-, technical-, or customer-centric.

Advisors usually receive stock options in the company they work with. Mentors may or may not be compensated. Coaches are typically compensated on a fee-for-service basis.

One of the biggest mistakes entrepreneurs make in choosing a mentor is basing their decision on a mentor's industry experience, rather than on the help and advice they themselves actually need. Sometimes entrepreneurs choose mentors who give them the reassurance they want, rather than the practical candor they need. For example, we have found that many early-stage companies correctly identify a market opportunity, but not necessarily the initial target customers. Moreover, they frequently lack an understanding of how to go about discovering, verifying, and validating their market opportunity. Mentors who understand the startup process, even though they may lack deep domain expertise, are often more valuable to a startup than those who possess domain expertise but lack an understanding of the challenges of early-stage startups.

Matching mentors is like arranging marriages."

– Viki Forrest

Viki Forrest

Viki Forrest is CEO of ANZA, an organization that helps Australian companies looking to enter the U.S. market or raise capital.

"Matching mentors to startup companies is like arranging marriages. Young entrepreneurs are keen to be mentored, but do not know what they need. In a good match, the entrepreneur and the mentor establish trust rapidly because they know they are right for each other.

"What makes mentoring work? The mentee must be mentor-able. And the personalities must work well together. Often, contrasting personalities click.

"The role of the mentor is not to be the VP of sales. Rather, it is to provide advice and counsel to the less-experienced CEO. Nor does a mentor necessarily bring technical expertise, or a list of contacts, though getting connected to people is incredibly important."

In seeking out mentors, we encourage entrepreneurs to find those experts who provide direct, no-bullshit feedback and who help them identify things they might have otherwise missed.

Large Corporations

One of the best-kept secrets in the Valley is the number of large corporations with significant activities here. We're not just talking about technology companies. The Valley also is home to large food producers, automotive manufacturers, and many consumer product goods companies.

These large corporations play multiple roles. They may be customers, partners, investors, or acquirers of startups, or all four. For example, Intel maintains a traditional venture capital fund. Siemens has an external innovation group that focuses on creating partnerships with promising startup companies. These startups can validate their value proposition with Siemens' business groups and then develop go-to-market partnerships and other business agreements.

Other corporations have innovation centers that help develop new technologies. And still others serve as limited partners in traditional venture funds. However, one of the more significant roles that large corporations play is as acquirers of venture-backed companies. Apple, Cisco, Facebook, Google, Microsoft, and IBM are all acquirers. Given that most venture-backed companies do not or cannot go public, these corporations serve a very important role in the Silicon Valley ecosystem.

Weather

Bay Area weather is great (except for the cold summers in San Francisco). This allows people to be outside, mingling at cafés and outdoor dining spots. While this may seem a small factor, it contributes significantly to the informal social interactions that are so important in the Valley, and it adds to the vitality and vibrancy of the region.

Airports

Not many places are served by three large international airports. San Francisco, San Jose, and Oakland airports allow people from around the world to get to Silicon Valley easily—and with a minimum number of connecting flights. Likewise, those living in the Bay Area have easy access to many other parts of the globe. And while some think of Silicon Valley as a self-contained business region, nothing could be further from the truth. Many companies have teams of engineers, customer-support personnel, manufacturing facilities, and customers scattered around the world.

❝ Silicon Valley is halfway between Europe and Asia, and close to Latin America. It's easy to do business anywhere in the world when you're based in Silicon Valley. ❞

– Mark White, White Summers Caffee & James

All the people and organizations listed above are important and visible parts of the ecosystem that makes Silicon Valley unique. Yet they make up only one piece of the puzzle. The Silicon Valley you can only experience, and the hidden Silicon Valley, are equally important in understanding how the Valley really works.

An aerial view of Silicon Valley

CHAPTER 3

The Silicon Valley You Must Experience

While many of the components of Silicon Valley that we described in Chapter 2—the people and the institutions—are clearly visible to the average visitor, they are only a part of what makes Silicon Valley unique. The Valley's success is also predicated on factors that are *experiential* in nature.

Here are some things we think are important for you to experience in Silicon Valley.

Identifying the Right People

The task that challenges entrepreneurs everywhere is that of identifying and connecting with the "right" people for their startups—team members, mentors and advisors, investors, and customers. Finding the right people can be achieved in one of two ways. The first is a proactive, step-by-step process that requires navigating a path to those people through your network. The second is what we fondly call *random, happy accidents*, or *serendipity*. Let's take a look at each of these approaches.

The *step-by-step process* for identifying the right people goes something like this. You begin by developing a profile of the kinds of people and companies you want to meet with. Who are the relevant people most likely to help you accomplish your goals? Which industry sector and what size of company are they in? Be thoughtful about whether the people you've identified are at the right levels in their respective organizations. Someone too high in an organization may not have the knowledge or visibility of the problem to help you, while someone too low may not have adequate awareness of their organization's needs. During this process, your initial idea of who the "right" people are will likely change as you start recognizing patterns and trends.

Once you have identified the kinds of people you want to meet with, you then have to navigate a path to them. To do this, you reach out to your circle of contacts (mentors, advisors, fellow entrepreneurs, lawyers). You ask them to help you identify specific individuals who closely match your profiles, and you ask to be introduced to those people. Your ability to recognize patterns—who fits your profile and who doesn't—will help speed things up.

> **❝ For people who come here from other places, the barrier to entry into the Silicon Valley network is surprisingly low. ❞**
>
> – Dave McClure, 500 Startups

Once you've succeeded in getting a meeting, your job is to determine if there is indeed a fit between your company and the people you're meeting with. You also want to elicit feedback about your ideas. And you want to capture suggestions on who else to meet with. Ideally, you'll secure a promise of several email introductions for the next set of contacts.

Here are some pointers to keep in mind for those meetings:

- Be polite, but persistent, in scheduling your meetings. Remember that punctuality and follow-through are keys to making a positive impression.

- Ask for advice and feedback, rather than trying to close the deal (unless the situation dictates otherwise).

- Listen more than you talk.

- Ask open-ended questions.

- Be prepared to answer questions and to address concerns. Don't get defensive.

- Ask for introductions to other people who might prove helpful.

- Ask how you can support and assist the person you're currently meeting with.

Over time, this process will help you develop a curated network of experienced people who can help you identify staffers, customers, investors, and partners.

In our experience, too many entrepreneurs fail to understand this process, and fail to recognize the importance of *physically* being in the Valley in order to work the process. We worked with one entrepreneur from Asia who had no idea who his target customers were in the U.S. He thought the best way to find out was simply to create a partnership with IBM or PriceWaterhouseCoopers and let them figure it out for him. But large companies such as these are not in the business of helping entrepreneurs identify and validate their initial target markets. Of course, they were not interested in doing this entrepreneur's job, nor was it their strong suit. The irony of this was that when pressed, the entrepreneur then identified a small Chinese restaurant chain he believed would be a good initial pilot customer. Unfortunately, the product offered far more features and capabilities than this restaurant could ever need. He would have saved a lot of energy had he spent time finding the right people in the Valley, eliciting their advice and then listening to what they had to say. Identifying the right size and type of organization is the first step in navigating to the right people.

The second approach to finding the right people—by *random, happy accidents*—is where randomness meets luck, what we call *serendipity*. In this approach, you attend events where you think the right people will be, or where you may meet people who can refer you to the right person, company, or resource.

As improbable as this may sound, it turns out that this is an excellent way to get connected. We have worked with dozens of entrepreneurs who've made connections this way while they were visiting Silicon Valley. This is because of the high density of people involved in technology in the Valley, most of whom have networks of contacts that are both broad and eclectic. There's no formula for how it works, but the following stories from Balazs Farago and Fabio Santini illustrate how it can successfully work.

> *"The lucky part was being in the right place at the right time."* – Balazs Farago

Balazs Farago

Balazs Farago is CEO of Real5D, an interactive 3D software platform that turns 3D models of real estate into interactive, walkable spaces.

"In May 2012 the company was running out of cash. I knew I had limited time to raise capital, and it was crucial to get financing in Silicon Valley. When I came to the Valley, I had only one contact—attorney Mark White—and I didn't know anyone else. We knocked on doors, pitched investors, and exchanged lots of business cards, but there was no guarantee of raising capital. We met investors at bars, lobbies, hotels, event venues, and Starbucks. Ten days into my stay—and close to the end of my visit—I met an investor from Double Rock at the Rosewood Hotel on Sand Hill Road in Menlo Park. The investor was having drinks with someone else, saw me using the Real5D product on my laptop, and started a conversation. That conversation turned into a meeting a few days later where we shook hands on a deal. The lucky part was being in the right place at the right time.

"I then went to Mark White and he agreed to be our Silicon Valley attorney. I explained that we had to complete the funding before I returned home to Hungary in a week. Mark worked quickly with the investor's attorney to complete the paperwork. They knew exactly what had to be done. I was impressed by how professional everyone was and how all the legal structures—terms and conditions—fell into place. I found myself in a business ecosystem full of people with a great deal of experience. Everything was here and nothing had to be reinvented. It was a very good experience."

"Connections can come from the most unexpected places. It's unbelievable." – Fabio Santini

Fabio Santini

Fabio Santini is founder and CEO of Neteye, a Brazilian-based startup providing workforce management software.

Fabio Santini frequently worked mornings at the artisanal coffee house Dharma Coffee in Mountain View. "I love it here. It's quiet and the coffee is good," he often says. In June 2015, Ed, the part-time barista, was behind the counter helping out the owner of Dharma coffee. As he was taking Santini's coffee order, he overheard Santini's conversation with an individual Santini had met through Founder Dating. Ed asked Santini if he wanted to meet his former boss from VMWare, who might have an interest in Neteye. Ed made an email intro that day, and one day later Santini and Ed's contact were sitting down for a meeting over coffee at Dharma's.

The following day, they met again, and this time Ed's contact brought someone who worked for Intel. Both loved the product and expressed strong interest in the company. As the meeting wound down, Santini asked how they might like to get involved. They suggested that they become either board members or advisors who would introduce Santini to investors. They also discussed how Santini could incorporate the company in the United States and transfer the intellectual property (IP) to a U.S. entity. And they talked about the possibility of making an investment in the company. What was supposed to be a one-hour meeting turned into much more.

"While they didn't say it openly," Santini remarks, "I believe they have the investment capital themselves. And what I expect now is to keep in touch with them. This was the best meeting I had after three months in Silicon Valley—and it wouldn't have happened in Brazil or anywhere else in the world."

We can't guarantee that if you show up at the Rosewood Hotel or Dharma Coffee you will be successful in finding the right person or in raising capital. What we *can* guarantee you is that being *present* in Silicon Valley gives you a greater chance of meeting the right people, whether through networking or *random, happy accidents.*

Honing Your Networking Skills

Networking events are a hallmark of Silicon Valley. Almost every day of the workweek, you can find events where entrepreneurs gather with other key people in the ecosystem. While agendas may include speakers, panels, or startup showcases, the organizers typically include time for participants to make connections with one another. Some events are "content free"—that is, they are gatherings for the sole purpose of networking.

> **"***People have a real interest in helping one another here.* **"**
>
> – Lene Sjorslev Schulze, 42 Associates

Going to events helps keep you connected. You stay visible and relevant. When we attend events, we catch up with people we know and get the latest updates about their current projects and activities. Those people frequently offer to make new introductions for us because they've met new people since we last saw them.

In addition to various kinds of get-togethers and meetups hosted by organizations such as Silicon Valley Forum, Silicon Vikings, and BayBrazil, there are large conferences—TechCrunch, Startup Grind, DEMO, TiE, AlwaysOn, Launch and DreamForce, for example—where thousands of people converge. Despite the inherent competition between startups in the same sector or market, camaraderie often develops at these gatherings; and information, insights, and leads are sometimes shared.

Networking isn't about collecting a large stack of business cards. Rather, it's about building business relationships and establishing trust. To build relationships, you need to learn more about an individual, identifying commonalities in background, outside interests, and personal connections. To establish trust, you need to be open and truthful about who you are, and to behave in a professional and appropriate manner. Successful networking is based on the assumption that when called on in the future, you will reciprocate in various ways, which can include offering access to your own network of contacts.

> *The whole ecosystem here is about sharing and connecting, yet there is no free lunch, as everybody says.*
>
> – Fabio Santini, Neteye

While people in Silicon Valley are open to networking, random requests to connect with people you don't know generally do not work. A warm introduction by a mutual contact is far more fruitful than an unsolicited request to connect via LinkedIn.

There are some essential steps you must take before you ask others to make introductions on your behalf. A clear statement of what your company does, why you want the meeting, and what the other person might get from meeting with you needs to be drafted and forwarded to the individual making the introduction on your behalf.

Once you've started to grow your network, maintaining it takes time and energy. And it turns out that LinkedIn *is a good way to keep connected*. You may wish to comment periodically on your contacts' updates, post updates of your own projects, acknowledge birthdays, forward articles or links of value, and follow up online with people you meet at networking events. You can also use LinkedIn to remain visible and relevant by updating your photo, or changing your header or title. If you have LinkedIn Premium, you can see who's viewed your profile and reach out to them.

> ❝ *Your network is all in one place. That makes it very hard to leave, and without that bridge you become kind of useless.* ❞
>
> – David Lee, SK Telecom

To keep your network growing, you may also want to approach your current contacts every six to twelve months and ask them if they have suggestions on new people you should meet. Of course, you'll want to offer to connect them with others who might be helpful to them. Over time, you will find certain people in your network more valuable than others; it's important to actively cultivate and maintain these relationships and to reciprocate regularly.

And while the Valley is densely populated, networks do overlap—so it's best not to disparage someone openly because that person may be a good friend of the person you're talking to.

> ❝ *Don't underestimate how well-networked people are in Silicon Valley.* ❞
>
> – Susan Lucas-Conwell, Innovation Catalyst

The ability to identify meaningful business contacts and to build strong business relationships is a key characteristic of successful Silicon Valley entrepreneurs. And the high density of startups, the mobility of workers, and a quid pro quo attitude all contribute to the creation of tightly connected networks of people here. However, it's also important to recognize that people in the Valley are very time-challenged. Sometimes it can take multiple attempts to get their attention. So be polite, yet persistent.

Taking Advantage of Pitch Competitions and Demo Days

Silicon Valley offers lots of pitch competitions. Pitching events are sponsored by a variety of organizations, from reputable companies to groups whose primary motive is to make money by charging fees to presenters or attendees. The caliber of judges at these events varies, as does the caliber of the attendees who actually show up. Some pitch competitions offer cash prizes.

Most of the incubators and accelerators in the Valley host demo days at the conclusion of their respective programs. Because these events are typically by-invitation-only, they attract higher-quality attendees.

Many people both inside and outside Silicon Valley think that pitch competitions are the *only* way to gain visibility and raise capital. While such competitions can increase visibility—pitching to an audience of fifty *key* people can be the equivalent of pitching to several hundred—pitch competitions are typically only a starting point in the process of raising money. When you pitch, you expand your pool of potential investors. The only downside to pitching events is that often a company is judged more on the *quality of the presentation* than on the *quality of the investment opportunity*.

Red Rock Cafe in Mountain View

"Following a form will not make you Shakespeare."

– Chris Yeh, PBWorks

Chris Yeh

Chris Yeh is an angel investor and VP of marketing at PBWorks.

"The pitch has become something of an art. Unfortunately, the pitch competition has become a test of how well you know the conventions of the art form. For example, the pitch formula at Y Combinator is: 'Let's talk about Mary. Mary has a problem...and this is where we come in.' By focusing on this formula, some presenters fail to present what is unique and special about their business. Following a form will not make you Shakespeare!

"Among an audience of investors, the question should be: Is this the best presentation of the day, or is this the best company to invest in? All too often, investors confuse the former with the latter."

Yeh tells the story of TrackR—a successful company in which he invested, run by a couple of engineering guys. The company was doing several million in revenue, but they were having trouble raising money because the founders weren't effective presenters.

"Lots of people think it's easy to raise money in Silicon Valley—but it's only easy if you've already raised money. For those who haven't, it is, in fact, very hard. Raising money in the Valley often involves more than rational decision-making. What you wear, how you speak, and how well you embody the role of a successful entrepreneur factors in. Personality flaws—coming off as arrogant, not coachable, or short-tempered—will cause investors to pass on investing in your company. And sometimes, not being a good presenter makes a difference—though it shouldn't.

"There's a stereotyping that goes on in Silicon Valley, very similar to the HBO TV show *Silicon Valley*. Somebody's the fat guy, somebody's the weird one with facial hair, and somebody's the Asian guy. Right or wrong, investors get so busy figuring out who is who that they don't spend enough time being thoughtful in their investing."

Coupa Cafe in Palo Alto

"The difference between a good pitch event and a bad one..." — Susan Lucas-Conwell

Susan Lucas-Conwell

Susan Lucas-Conwell, former CEO of SVForum, now works as an innovation catalyst for large corporations and as a mentor to startups.

"What's the difference between a good pitch event and a bad one? It's all about the quality of the organizers, the audience, and an understanding of the outcome. SVForum puts on a quarterly investor forum where ten to twelve companies pitch to a room of sixty to eighty angel and venture investors. That's one example of a good event. There are numerous others put on by reputable organizations, including several universities. In those events, there's a cachet to winning.

"A bad event? Bad events are often put on by service providers or other for-profit groups. The motive of these organizers is to attract clients or to make money—not necessarily to get your company financed. Who shows up? Students, other service providers, and job seekers, many of whom want to visit the cool places where these events are often held—Facebook, Google, Salesforce.com, and Twitter, to name a few. Who else attends? Junior associates at venture funds who are measured by the number of deals they source, not necessarily by the quality of the deal. Other attendees include faux VCs and faux angels (that is, those who don't have any funds to invest). These days, out-of-work executives, failed entrepreneurs, and failed 'somethings' often rebrand themselves as angel investors. They don't actually invest and they often waste an entrepreneur's time.

"Is there value to this kind of event? Surprisingly, yes. While the judges may be second-rate and the winner really doesn't win anything, these events can provide a venue to practice—or just to watch others perform. And such events give entrepreneurs the opportunity to learn about the culture of Silicon Valley, and, of course, to network. They are also good places to do competitive analysis. But to raise capital, these events are unlikely to produce results.

"Beyond pitch events, there are other ways to source capital. For startups whose products or services fit with an existing company's distribution channel or customer base, the corporate investment arm of those companies may be a better source for financing. Verizon and Orange both have funds to invest in startups working in the wireless area. Generally, these startups need to have both product and some customer feedback or validation before corporate investors will talk to them."

One of the best ways to learn how to pitch effectively is to watch others and analyze how they might improve their pitches. You will need to develop your own presentation style and rehearse it until you know it cold. And, as you get feedback, you must continue to make improvements to the presentation.

While there are numerous books, seminars, and training programs that discuss how to pitch in great detail, here's our short list of things that distinguish great presentations:

- **Tell a story.** It's the most powerful way to present your business.

- **Keep it simple.** Your presentation should be easy to understand by your audience (and your mom). If your business is too hard to explain, you need to figure out a different way to present it.

- **Keep it short.** Fewer slides with simple design and minimal text are best. We have included in Appendix B our outline for a ten-slide presentation. Use it as a guide only. Your presentation needs to be tailored to the specifics of your company as well as your audience.

- **Determine the purpose of the presentation.** Often you'll be making a short presentation to see if there's a fit between your company and an investor. If there is interest, you'll be invited to give a more in-depth presentation. Most entrepreneurs have both short and long versions of their presentations.

- **Understand your audience.** Make sure you know whom you are presenting to, and what their backgrounds are.

- **Pay attention to the allotted time.** A three-minute presentation is different in content from a twenty-minute one. Too often we see entrepreneurs trying to fit a twenty-minute presentation in the three minutes they are allotted. It doesn't work.

- **Focus on the business.** Eighty percent of the presentation should be on the business, and only 20 percent on the technology or product, unless it is strictly a product-only showcase.

- **Do not read your slides.** Instead, rehearse your presentation so that you know it by heart.

- **Project confidence and credibility.** How you carry yourself and how you respond to questions are important in developing trust among potential customers and investors. Maintain eye contact. Do not pace while you present.

- **Ask for questions.** They should be part of your overall presentation. Provide short answers, and slightly longer explanations as necessary.

- **Manage the Q&A session.** Learn how to bridge from the question asked to the answer you want to give.

- **Don't be defensive.** Listen to criticism and address issues raised.

- **Be positive.** Present your company in a positive light, but don't misrepresent and do not lie.

There is so much talk about pitching that you might think it is replacing soccer, baseball, or football as our most popular spectator sport. It isn't. While it's important to know what to pitch and how to pitch, your passion and ability to execute on your idea are far more important to building a successful company.

And here's the list we've compiled—after hearing thousands of entrepreneurs make their pitches—of the most common mistakes we've observed:

- **Missing or incomplete title slide** – This slide needs to include the company name, the presenter's name and title, key contact information, and ideally an appropriate tagline.

- **Failure to describe the purpose of your presentation** – Be sure that you explain why you are presenting and what you want from your audience. This should be done verbally, not necessarily with a separate slide.

- **Failure to state what your company does** – Explain verbally, in one to two sentences, what your company does and for whom.

- **Disconnect between slides and verbal presentation** – Make sure your slides are consistent with the story you're telling, and that they match the purpose of your pitch. Also, we see too many slides that are illegible because the font is too small, the color is too hard to see, or the slide has too many words or too much detail.

- **Failure to clearly identify a specific initial customer profile** – Present your initial customer profile narrowly, with specifics around industry, geography, size of company. Narrow, narrow, narrow.

- **Inappropriate level of detail on the team slide** – Here we've seen both too many and too few words. We prefer simply to see job titles, with logos that show prior employers.

- **Failure to clearly articulate the pain point** – It's important to explain the economic cost of the problem you're trying to solve. Why must it get solved, and for whom?

- **Missing or obtuse value proposition** – Be sure to include a clear, concise description of the value your company's solution delivers.

- **Lack of clarity on business model** – Present your revenue and business models clearly (for example, revenue per typical customer).

- **Inadequate or missing competitive analysis** – Do not include a grid of features, benefits, and check marks, nor 2X2 quadrants. Instead, find and communicate a unique positioning versus the competition.

- **Incomplete go-to-market plan** – Frequently, we don't see specifics about how the company will close customers and build revenues, that is, the "what" and "how" of building the business.

- **Inadequate market research** – Do not show a lack of understanding about the industry, target market, competitors, or how business is done. Do your homework.

- **Failure to tailor presentation** – A lack of understanding of the audience and their objectives makes the presentation less relevant and compelling to them.

Cafe Borrone in Menlo Park

"Winning provides instant recognition, but you need to know how to leverage it." – Zia Yusuf

Zia Yusuf

Zia Yusuf is partner and managing director at BCG, a consulting firm, and the former CEO of Streetline, a venture-backed company.

Two months after Zia Yusef joined Streetline, the company won the IBM Global Smartcamp competition. Overnight, this event put Streetline on the map, with extensive publicity and support from IBM. "It provided instant recognition," Yusuf remarks, "but you need to know how to leverage it in your marketing and public relations. Otherwise, it can fizzle quickly."

Yusuf describes how the partnership with IBM provided the company with huge benefits. "A lot of people in the ventures group helped to shepherd us through the corporation and provide leverage to Streetline. They helped the company with marketing, customer development, and enhancements to the technology. We were also invited to events and conferences, which gave us the opportunity to present at the top tier to IBM partners. IBM definitely helped with our go-to-market efforts.

"But it was much tougher to engage the IBM salesforce to sell Streetline products. The biggest hurdle was the incentive system. The Streetline products had lower median selling prices than other products sold by the sales team, and since the sales reps had a $3 to $5 million annual quota, it was hard to get them to spend time on Streetline products. And over time, the Smart Cities initiative within IBM faded, people moved on or retired, and it became tough getting the attention of the new folks."

Participating in the Café Culture

There are numerous corner cafés and coffee shops throughout the Bay Area where you can see entrepreneurs discussing their companies with investors, prospective employees, lawyers, and other service professionals. In Silicon Valley, these meetings often occur at certain well-known cafés and coffee shops—Café Barrone, Dharma Coffee, Coupa Café, Red Rock Café, and various local Peet's and Philz, among others. Since this practice is not as common in other business regions around the world, we are sometimes asked why so many meetings—particularly initial ones—take place in these cafés. Here's what we know.

> *Go to Red Rock Café in Mountain View. Listen to the conversations around you. People are pitching— they're talking about products and partnerships all the time. It's amazing.*
>
> – Fabio Santini, Neteye

Holding a meeting in a café is informal—and informality is the hallmark of the Valley. And, by the way, showing up for a meeting at a café in a three-piece suit labels you an *outsider*. Jeans and a sport shirt will help you fit in better.

Despite the fact that cafés are notoriously noisy and crowded, meeting at a café can offer more privacy than meeting at the office. It's no big deal to meet someone for coffee, but to bring an outsider to the office suggests that the topic of conversation is serious. What's more, people may overhear snippets of your discussion.

Café meetings can be as short as twenty minutes or as long as an hour— depending on the interest of the people around the table. When an idea is of interest, people stay longer. When it's not, they can conveniently excuse themselves since there is no food to wait for and no meal to sit through. And, in a funny way, a café meeting, while demonstrating interest, communicates a lower expectation for follow-up or follow-through.

Finally, unlike an office or conference room, a café is a neutral zone where everyone looks and acts "equal" (though we know that's not really the case).

Meetings do take place in offices and conference rooms, especially when a white board, quiet discussion, and more time are required.

After the initial meeting, there's an order to the kinds of meetings that follow: coffee, lunch, drinks, dinner, invitation to a sporting event, and so forth. Each of these signals a different level of interest between parties.

Typically meetings take place between 8 a.m. and 6 p.m. However, when interest is high, people are often willing to meet for an early breakfast or into the evening. Rarely will people meet for dinner unless the relationship is important, or there's a good rationale, such as conflicting schedules. A lunch meeting is more typical, as is a drink after work. An invitation to a sporting event is less common.

Business is done everywhere in Silicon Valley—in the car, on the street, in cafés, from home—and frequently across time zones.

Embracing the Constant Change

Silicon Valley has systems in place that keep things flowing, changing, and growing in new directions and in unexpected ways. We cannot tell you exactly why it works, but it does. It operates at just the right pace—not so fast that the players in the ecosystem get lost, and not so slow that things get boring.

But along with this freewheeling process comes a natural cycle of boom and bust. Those who have lived here for decades have seen great times and bad, too much money and too little. Windows open for "liquidity"—a Silicon Valley term that means selling your company or having it listed on a public exchange—and then they close. As with any well-oiled engine, sometimes things go well, and sometimes they get out of alignment. Getting used to this roller coaster ride is a very important lesson for anyone who frequents or lives in the Valley. The cycles are natural and will continue to occur.

> *Silicon Valley is continually being reinvented. We make it up as we go along. And this process creates a great deal of vibrancy.*
>
> – Mark White, White Summer Caffee & James

What was hot yesterday is not today. And what investors are interested in today will likely change tomorrow. Clean tech, wind power, and batteries were once big news in Silicon Valley. Then it was apps, and B2B (business-to-business) and enterprise software. Then SaaS (software as a service) became big. Then wearable technology grabbed people's attention. All these took place, individually, within about 24 months. If you're going to do business in Silicon Valley, you have to keep pace and move quickly. And if you leave and come back in six months, it's bound to be a changed place. The ideas, interests, and buzz will all be different.

We *embrace and celebrate* this constant change. But more important, we expect it. There are always new companies, new people, and new ideas that keep things interesting.

The Silicon Valley you experience is as important as the Silicon Valley you can see. While it can be viewed and appreciated from afar, you only gain value and perspective when you actively participate. So show up. Be part of our community, participate in the events, attend pitch competitions, and experience the Valley. Participation can help make you a more effective entrepreneur.

CHAPTER 4

Hidden Silicon Valley

Like any other place, Silicon Valley has a particular history, culture, and style of operating—all of which affect how business gets done here. Let us give you some examples. There is a pioneering, slightly rebellious spirit in the Valley—one in which asking for forgiveness is acceptable, and often preferable to asking for permission. There is an openness that encourages collaboration and sharing, but there is also a reluctance to give brutally honest feedback unless it is specifically requested. And there is a belief that everyone will take you at face value, though you should know that people do perform reference checks on anyone they are considering working with or investing in—and you may never know.

Your success in the Valley has a lot to do with understanding the culture and norms here. In this chapter, we discuss the non-obvious things—what we call the Hidden Silicon Valley—that help create and define the business ecosystem. Use it as a starting point for getting yourself acclimated. The Valley rewards quick learners.

Core Values

Silicon Valley encourages people to be optimistic and think big, but there is a point at which the feasibility of an outlying idea or business plan will be questioned. A big idea and a good story can get you just so far. Do not underestimate the value of actually building product, closing sales, and scaling your business. Results do matter in the Valley.

> *Tell an Australian about the global ambitions for your startup and they'll tell you a hundred reasons why it won't work. Tell an American—or better yet, tell someone from Silicon Valley—and they'll find a hundred ways to help you make it work.*
>
> – Viki Forrest, ANZA Technology Network

We also talk about "paying it forward" here—and we actually practice it. But when someone fails to reciprocate, or when someone we've referred to a colleague embarrasses us, the door slams shut—often without explanation.

On the surface, there is a sense of informality and equality in Silicon Valley. This image, which is reinforced by casual attire and open offices at many companies, is often projected in the media. But the reality is different. There actually is a hierarchy. While management may seek input, decisions are made at the senior level. And when it comes to allocating stock options or divvying up proceeds once a company is sold, decisions are made at the highest levels—and the pot doesn't get split equally.

Finally, while there is a view that Californians, including those of us in Silicon Valley, are more laid back than others throughout the United States, in fact businesspeople here have a work-hard, play-hard approach that permeates the startup world.

> *The kind of ambition you feel here, the kind of urgency you feel here, is very hard to find outside of Silicon Valley. When I'm here, I feel like things are happening in real time, like my Twitter feed, versus getting something in the mail. You're living and experiencing it now.*
>
> – Derek Anderson, Startup Grind

Behavior

If you're likable, people here are generally more willing to forgive any faux pas you may make. By contrast, if you are not personable and rather unlikable, no matter what you do correctly, you may not be successful.

Several years ago we ran into an entrepreneur who was arrogant, didn't listen, and had a superiority complex. Otherwise, he was a nice guy! He had won a prize at SXSW, and he thought that this achievement alone was enough for him to raise capital, regardless of the feasibility of his business. He found it really tough to get anything done because others who interacted with him had the same negative reaction that we did. Being likeable goes a long way in Silicon Valley, as it does in most other parts of the world.

Time is a precious commodity in the Valley, so it's important not to waste others' time. In a meeting, have a clear business purpose in mind and get to the point quickly. And since organizations in Silicon Valley are complex, recognize that decision-making may also be complex. Rarely does the CEO of a large company get involved in operational-level reviews and decisions. Sure, your product is cool, but it isn't likely that you'll be discussing it with Larry Page at Google. Understand that it takes time to get to the individuals who actually make the decisions.

> *Here you start on time and you finish on time. In Brazil, sometimes we spend two to three hours talking and the conversation doesn't go anywhere. The icebreakers alone sometimes take a half an hour.*
>
> – Fabio Santini, Neteye

How you interact in a business meeting is important, too. Assuming a demeanor that's too informal won't work, nor will crude jokes or TMI (too much information). Being professional, genuine, and warm is what's called for. And sending a short follow-up email thanking people for their time is the norm here.

Communication Style

In the Valley communication styles are direct, brief, and to the point. This is reflected in simple things, such as how quickly you respond to emails (within twenty four hours is normal), and how you answer a question (the answer first, then a short explanation, not the other way around—and certainly the answer should take no more than a minute or two to read). Long emails and too-frequent emails are not okay. And of course, take the time to spell the name of your email recipient properly, and make sure your grammar is correct.

Often, as an entrepreneur, you don't have complete information or answers with which to take action or make decisions. Without sufficient information, there is a tendency to *not* respond to the emails or telephone calls related to that issue. An alternate approach would be to get back to the person with, "I don't know the answer yet but should have one in X weeks." This is much better than simply ignoring the second, third or fourth email.

In some regions of the world, an entrepreneur doesn't present company financials to a potential investor until the third or fourth meeting. In the Valley, it's expected that all information, albeit brief, will be presented in the initial meetings. Providing more detail than is appropriate should be avoided. And sharing information that is not on topic can be distracting and hurt your credibility.

Sometimes non-American entrepreneurs stumble because of terminology or nomenclature. For instance, Australians need to ban the word *scheme* from their vocabulary, especially when used in conjunction with the word *business*, since a scheme in the U.S. connotes something illegal. We say *revenue*, not *turnover*. And when using numerals, we put a comma between every three significant digits, not a period—so four thousand is expressed as 4,000. A period is used only to denote fractions of a dollar.

The media are often guilty of portraying Silicon Valley as a place where buzzwords are the norm. Certainly, some people here overuse terminology, but most of us who live and work here try to avoid buzzwords because of their generic nature. Describing your company as a "cloud-enabled, mobile, social media platform for gen-X'ers" may be accurate, but it's unlikely that others will really understand what you do—since there are hundreds of companies that could conceivably fit this broad description. A good test for figuring out whether you're using buzzwords is to write your *elevator pitch*—a few short sentences that describe the problem you solve and the customers you reach—and test it out on your grandmother. If she understands, then you've achieved clarity in communicating what you do.

Non-compete Contracts

Many large companies throughout the U.S. require employees to sign non-compete contracts so that when an employee quits, he or she cannot take trade secrets, customer contact lists, or knowledge of the company's strategies to a competitor. Some states, including Massachusetts, honor non-compete agreements. But these agreements are rarely enforceable in California, a situation that many believe increases job mobility and creates a favorable environment for new startups. In fact, a number of VCs have pointed to this fact as the reason why Massachusetts has so few entrepreneurs who have left large- and medium-size employers to start their own companies.

California-based Cisco Systems is a good example here. Dozens of former Cisco employees have started companies that compete directly or indirectly with this networking giant. And Cisco, for its part, has directly invested in some of the non-competitive startups, later acquiring those companies outright.

Lack of Interest in Lifetime Employment

Rarely do workers expect—or want—lifetime employment in Silicon Valley. In fact, most workers view a constant movement between jobs as a way to gain valuable experience, to increase their networks, and to find their next challenges. And employers view experience at numerous companies on a job seeker's résumé as a desirable asset.

And there's one more benefit here: Since few people are expecting to stay at a company for a lifetime, job seekers do not feel they are taking that much more risk in joining a startup than they might in accepting a job at a company like Hewlett-Packard, once considered a top employer offering long-term, stable jobs.

Geographic Constraints

We often think of Silicon Valley as a big, little place. The region—which is bounded by San Francisco, San Jose, the East Bay, and the Pacific Ocean—is the fifth largest metropolitan area in the U.S., with a population of over 7 million. California is also the seventh largest economy in the world. However, the San Francisco Bay Area is divided into different parts by numerous bridges. The city of San Francisco has its own startup community, as do the mid-Peninsula, Palo Alto, and San Jose areas. The East Bay and Berkeley, too, have their own communities. Physical barriers and the resulting traffic congestion effectively concentrate entrepreneurs in a number of relatively small geographic areas.

How do you learn these things? It takes time—and sometimes, it helps to have an advisor or even a sherpa who lives and works in the Valley. In the end, it doesn't matter *how* you learn, it just matters *that* you learn these things—and that you learn them quickly.

CHAPTER 5

The Silicon Valley Mindset

In this chapter, we will take you through the *Silicon Valley mindset*, the region's unique way of viewing, evaluating, and growing businesses. But before doing so, it's useful to review what we have described thus far in this journey through Silicon Valley. In the first four chapters, we explored the importance of the region—including what you see, what you experience, and what's hidden in plain sight in the Valley. We hope this core foundation of content helps you understand and appreciate the *what* of Silicon Valley.

The second half of the book will take you through the *how* of the Valley—how we approach building companies. The best travel experiences usually occur when you have the benefit of someone local who can help you interpret what you see and provide context. By giving you not only the *what*, but also the *how* of Silicon Valley, we will empower you to think and act like an insider. These insights will make you better connected, more effective as a communicator, and ultimately more successful in navigating the Valley.

As much as Silicon Valley is a physical place, it is also way of doing business and a set of best practices. More important, the region has a unique perspective and disciplined approach to assessing, building, and growing companies. This is what we define as the *Silicon Valley mindset*.

Everyone involved in the startup ecosystem here typically views and evaluates a startup in a similar way. The Silicon Valley approach is both thoughtful and strategic, and most of the businesses that are started here are planned and built in a systematic way. In our experience, while some companies do not follow this approach, sooner or later most do. This is in contrast to places outside Silicon Valley where the building of a business is more opportunistic in nature.

> *People in Silicon Valley—entrepreneurs, investors, bankers, lawyers—all speak the same language of business here. Entrepreneurship is our common frame of reference.*
>
> – Lene Sjorslev Schulze, 42 Associates

Understanding the Silicon Valley Mindset

Four key components make up the Silicon Valley mindset:

- **Valley View** – The Valley view is just that: a 360° assessment of a given company, the team, the market opportunity, and its business model. This practice is shared by entrepreneurs, prospective employees, customers, partners, and venture investors. While each constituent may focus on a particular aspect of the company—such as the entrepreneurs' focus on vision and urgency, customers' and partners' assessment of value proposition, and investors' preoccupation with the market opportunity and the team's ability to execute—collectively the constituents understand that all these factors will contribute to creating a high-growth, global company. And the ultimate goal of this value creation is to turn the company, at the right time, into cold, hard cash. For Silicon Valley companies, planning an exit is as important as planning their entrance; it is an integral part of a business plan and an absolute requirement for venture investors. If you can't get liquidity, there's no point in starting a company and raising capital.

  It's fair to acknowledge that a small, but increasing, number of companies are being started for social good and double bottom line.

In such cases, the objectives of founders and investors differ from the norm, and creating financial gain is not the overall goal. Yet in general, Silicon Valley is not interested in creating or building small, slow-growth, local or regional businesses; nor is it interested in lifestyle businesses that generate profits for their owners and may be then passed down to family members.

- **Problem/Solution Identification** – We have met entrepreneurs all over the world who focus on building a product, rather than on solving a problem for a particular market or customer. But in Silicon Valley, we look at problem/solution long before we look at product/market fit.

Addressing the problem/solution issue requires identifying the problem, and ensuring that it is significant enough that customers are willing to pay for a solution *today*. The solution must have a clear, compelling economic value to the customer. And it must solve the problem in an efficient, user-friendly manner, with strong differentiation from other solutions. Finally, the product must create barriers to entry for other competitors.

Savvy founders deal with the problem/solution issue *before* they have built a product or launched a service. They take the time to do the necessary homework ahead of determining the product/market fit.

Cisco Systems in San Jose

"No Swiss army knives here." – John Scull

John Scull

John Scull is a venture capitalist at Southern Cross Venture Partners.

"Silicon Valley is different from other markets where early fundraising is driven by brokers without regard to the kind of investors needed. In Silicon Valley, investors expect that the company CEO will contact them directly, and that the company has done its homework to ensure that it fits with the venture investor's investment profile.

"And there are other differences between U.S. markets and other places. In smaller markets, you have to be like a Swiss Army knife. That is, you have to go after multiple related markets since the general market isn't big enough. In the U.S., companies tend to be deeply focused on products for one market. Today everybody tries out a beta before launching a general release—so it's always a soft rollout.

"But if you make mistakes in a less competitive market, you can still survive. In Silicon Valley, the bar is high—so you need to be perfect in execution. Most failures come from being too early or too late to market. Better to be too early—you can moderate the cash burn. If you find few early adopters, you simply need patience."

- **Product/Market Fit** – The hardest part of the process is finding the right market fit for your product or service. Rarely are early-stage startups able to figure the product/market fit until they have interacted with customers. In many ways, the task of the startup is to experiment until the management team discovers what works. Most entrepreneurs go through this process. The lucky ones figure things out before they run out of time and money, while the others don't, and fail. The entire

Silicon Valley ecosystem considers experimentation and iteration a normal process for building and scaling companies.

During this phase, a mock-up, prototype, or *lite* version of the product is created and presented to customers for feedback and validation. In addition to experimenting, this process requires using one's curated network to find the right initial customers. The challenge is not just finding customers who need the product; it is in finding customers who are also *willing to buy from a startup*.

> ❝ *Finding out what doesn't work is really valuable.* ❞
>
> – Balazs Farago, Real5D

The team uses market feedback to refine the product, or to redefine the initial target customer. Then it goes back out into the market to see if sales can be closed. If target customers don't buy, the team spends time listening to their objections and identifying recurring patterns as to why they don't buy.

In the Valley, we also maintain a very tight focus on both the speed and the precision of execution. Our focus on finding the right people, the right technologies, and the right resources forces us to offload, outsource, and even ignore those things that are not in the critical path.

To have a viable business—a defined, repeatable, and scalable one that generates revenues from a global market—Silicon Valley focuses on startups that can disrupt existing industries, replace incumbents, or create totally new markets.

> ❝ *Many companies, such as Uber and AirBnB, are not creating new markets. They are simply resectioning existing markets. There's only so much you can take out of these markets.* ❞
>
> – Chris Yeh, PBWorks

In a perfect world, you get the process right the first time. In the real world, a great deal of iteration is required. It's better to complete the experimentation and iteration processes early. In doing so, you're more likely to raise capital—and at a higher valuation.

> *"Product traction and market traction are the lenses through which we judge a team."* – Dave McClure

Dave McClure

Dave McClure is the founding partner of 500 Startups.

Dave McClure has been doing early-stage seed investment for over fifteen years. The 500 Startups team has traveled extensively in its search for great entrepreneurs and companies. Today, more than half of its 1,000+ investments are outside the U.S. McClure shares some of the perceptions of Silicon Valley from those outside the region.

"Often there's a perception among outsiders that Silicon Valley is on another level—and that they can't play on that level. They put Silicon Valley on such a high pedestal that they develop an insecurity complex. And then international investors come to believe that their local entrepreneurs suck relative to Silicon Valley.

"When you first come here, you're in awe—sometimes too much so. But after a while, you acclimate and begin to think they're good, but I'm just like them. That's when you really step up your game.

"Lots of entrepreneurs think they need to have an NDA (nondisclosure agreement) before they meet with a venture capitalist; they're worried that VCs are going to steal their ideas. Many also feel that they need to create really long business plans with five-year revenue projections. It's possible that some investors here do care about those things, but revenue projections don't really matter until businesses are in later stages of development. Most of the companies that we're investing in are so speculative that having any kind of projections beyond six to twelve months out is kind of foolish. We actually prefer six- to twelve-month expense projections over three- to five-year revenue projections. And what we really prefer to see is a functional prototype, and some early customer usage data.

"There's also a perception that the story— the big idea—is what people need to pitch. Some investors may care about that. But we care about traction to date, and what you have done so far. I don't care if you think you're going to build a huge business or not. It's great that you have ambition, but you could be a really great liar, or a storyteller. We ask: Do you have a functional product? Have you gotten it out the door? Are customers paying for it? Can you show month-over-month growth for the last three, six or twelve months? Do you have previous product successes? And have you sold a small project or company before? Most of our due diligence is historical—backward looking, not forward looking. Product traction and market traction are the lenses through which we judge a team."

- **Value Creation** – By "value creation" we don't mean winning a pitch competition, nor do we mean raising significant venture capital for a concept on paper. The term *doesn't* refer to the valuation an investor places on a private company; in fact, such a valuation doesn't necessarily reflect what the company is potentially worth. Value is based on the caliber of the team; its ability to achieve milestones; the company's market presence, revenues, and profits; and the partnerships and distribution agreements in place.

In Silicon Valley, value creation leverages venture capital financing to accelerate both product development and sales and marketing ahead of the revenue ramp. This is done both to build market share quickly and to preempt competition. Silicon Valley companies frequently outsource noncritical functions such as accounting, human resources, and legal work as ways of keeping the company focused on the essential aspects of value creation, including product development and sales traction.

Finding the right people—employees, customers, mentors, and investors—is essential to growing and scaling a company. Silicon Valley relies on networking and *random, happy accidents*, as described in Chapter 3, to facilitate finding the right people. Virtually, everyone in the Valley's tech community gets out of the office and networks on a frequent basis. We network to find people and resources, and when we're not looking, we find the unexpected. There is no substitute for meeting people in person.

Now comes the hard part—the really hard part. It's not glamorous, and it's not often fun. It's a numbers game, and it takes a lot of blocking and tackling. You contact many prospective customers, and only a few bother to return your call or reply to your email, even though you were introduced to them by a mutual contact. And out of those you actually talk to, only a few actually turn into customers. And the next day, you get up and do it all over again.

At the same time, the key person you spent months cultivating and recruiting for your management team winds up taking a job at another hot startup, or Google makes an offer that person can't refuse. Or the integration work that was supposed to be completed in two weeks is stalled, with no end in sight—largely because the customer has reorganized and staff has turned over. Or a venture-backed competitor just announced a new version of its product at a major conference and the product directly competes with yours. Or you hear back from the board that your company isn't making the progress necessary to close a financing before the money runs out.

Yet somehow you close multiple customer deals, the product integration work gets completed, and you figure out how to navigate the new competitive threat. Every day is different. Every day is challenging. Building value in a company only appears easy in hindsight.

Google campus in Mountain View

"Customers aren't stupid." – Bill Grosso

Bill Grosso

Bill Grosso is the founder and CEO of Scientific Revenues, a venture-backed company that provides dynamic pricing for digital purchases.

"Impatience is a bad habit," Bill Grosso says about the challenges in getting customer traction. "You have to do a lot of groundwork before you start a company and build your product, and it's a mistake to hurry the process. First, you need to figure out who your target customers are. You need to identify fifty potential customers. Then you need to formulate five hypothetical products—and test them on those customers. Pattern recognition works here: Keep going until you see a pattern emerge.

"Once you think you've identified the right product, then the question becomes: How do you build a product that works not just for the first customer, but also for the first twenty? The reality is that the first twenty customers are each unique—so don't overpromise what you will deliver. Engineering slips; a four-month project can lag; and pretty soon you have a seven-month project. Tell your customers, because their bullshit detector is very high. Customers aren't stupid.

"When it comes to talking to potential customers, I use a low-key sales pitch. I don't go to a potential customer and use hyperboles or make outlandish claims. I make it educational—so that when they talk with me, they get valuable information regardless of whether they buy or not. Also, when I pitch I never schedule back-to-back meetings; if people are interested, they will give me more than the thirty minutes that was originally allotted for the meeting, and I always want to take advantage of that.

"Getting customer traction takes scheduling twenty to thirty customer conversations a week—and 90 percent of the people you talk to will be unenthusiastic. Do not take it personally. Instead, listen carefully, as they will give you important feedback—and sometimes leads. In fact, most leads come from failed sales calls. You can never know everyone, so you need evangelists to help you find customers! I try to create evangelists, whether they buy my product or not.

"It is important to know when to stop selling, too. When people don't believe the product will work, keep selling. But when they say that the issue you solve isn't a problem for them, then give up.

"Do you go after big companies or small ones? Surprisingly, large companies often move faster than smaller companies. Small companies will often keep saying yes for six months—and then do nothing. Some small companies have a perpetual inability to prioritize beyond their next crisis.

"Finally, when you are planning your sales strategy, remember that you cannot require people to change in too many ways. A good example is Segway, [self-balancing personal transporter]: The company developed compelling technology, but the only market it found was mall cops and tourists. It never caught on with our aging population—which really does need solutions for increased mobility. All too often we overestimate people's willingness to change."

In addition to the Silicon Valley mindset, here are a number of best practices that Valley entrepreneurs employ to help their startups succeed.

- **Support Startups** – Over decades, Silicon Valley has organized itself in a rather unique manner to serve and support the needs of entrepreneurs. We have specialized service professionals, and well-connected and tightly networked communities with many common bonds. The Valley offers a highly collaborative environment for startups, as well as much potential for cooperation between startups and large companies.

  By contrast, in many other regions of the world, being an entrepreneur means choosing a lonely—sometimes solitary—path, one in which the entrepreneur frequently lacks supporters who might help make the journey easier.

> " *Should a company locate in Silicon Valley? If it's a software and technology business, and most of the capital and talent is here, then yes. If there's no technology involved, there are plenty of other areas that may be better suited to building the business.* "

> – Viki Forrest, ANZA Technology Network

We have already mentioned that lawyers are important players in the Silicon Valley ecosystem. In addition to providing legal advice, contract documents, and other services, they frequently provide value by connecting startups to investors. Even the way they structure their compensation reflects their understanding of the startup reality. Savvy Silicon Valley attorneys understand that most startups don't have much cash in the beginning, so they often defer some portion of their fees until after the company receives its first round of financing.

We mentioned this deferred compensation plan to an attorney in France some years ago, and he was aghast. And when we pressed him about adapting his business model to the realities of startups' needs, he confessed that startups were probably not his ideal target market. Obviously, he simply saw himself as a provider of services and expertise, rather than as an active participant in the startup process.

One of the unique advantages of working with Silicon Valley investors is that many were previous company founders themselves, and they have knowledge and understanding of the startup process. As a result, they bring advice to the startup, and they are generally thoughtful about how they structure their investments so that founders remain motivated. Investors are in it for the long haul, with the goal of creating large, successful companies.

Silicon Valley has hundreds of accelerators, incubators, and shared office spaces. They provide workspace, community, and varying levels of advice and mentoring. Like the lawyers and investors, they can connect entrepreneurs to others in the Valley, including service professionals, investors, universities, trade associations, mentors and advisors, and often even potential customers.

- **Help Required** – Startups go through many different stages of growth and development. One of the unique aspects of Silicon Valley is that you can find specialized people and resources to address the needs of a startup at each of those stages. Need a bookkeeper when the company is just three people and the dog? It's here. When you've grown enough to need a part-time CFO, that person is also here. Launching your first product? You can work with a PR agency instead of hiring a full-time communications person. It's all here in Silicon Valley.

Silicon Valley also has many people with the skills and willingness to be startup mentors. Incubators, accelerators, and shared workspaces often maintain lists of people who function in these roles. Some of the lists are better curated than others. And there are other ways to find quality mentors, including attending events; networking; asking for referrals from lawyers, investors, and your own diaspora; and connecting with others on your own. Regardless of how you find a mentor, make sure that person is a good match for you and your needs.

At each stage of a company's life, resource people exist to help you move your company to the next level. Many will structure their fees structure (cash, equity, or a combination) according to the stage of growth your company is experiencing, as well as its ability to pay. In other words, they share the startup experience.

- **Constant Change** – Things both move and change very quickly in Silicon Valley. What was a hot game yesterday is not today. And what investors are interested in today may be different tomorrow. If you're going to do business in Silicon Valley, you have to keep pace and move quickly. If you leave and come back six months later, the Valley is bound to be a different place. The ideas, interest, buzz, and direction will likely all be quite different.

- **Speed and Intensity** – Organizing for speed in execution and decision making, responding in a timely manner to customer requests or crises, and being nimble are all-important attributes of the more successful Silicon Valley startups. Time is of the essence here, and rarely are there enough resources to do everything that a startup must do in the available time. A fast, nimble startup team must be ready to do whatever is necessary. Since startups often grapple with finding the right customer and market opportunity, a startup must move quickly and efficiently either to validate a market or to eliminate it and hunt for another.

To further their efficiencies, many Silicon Valley companies move the decision making process as far down in the organization as possible, and keep teams small, which gives them the freedom to test and iterate.

> *"It's insane how fast things move here!"*
>
> – Lene Sjorslev Schulze, 42 Associates

- **Open and Transparent** – In Silicon Valley, we are more open and transparent about a given company, its products, its progress, and its company financials than business people are in other regions of the world. When an entrepreneur is looking for help or guidance, the subject of money and financing is openly discussed. So please don't take it personally when we ask questions such as "How much money do you have left in the bank?" or "What's the equity split among partners and founders?" These questions are not meant to be personal or offensive. It's just business.

In a number of companies in Silicon Valley, the management team has taken openness and transparency quite far. In those companies, practices vary but they may include giving all employees access to board-level presentations, to peer performance reviews, and even to every employee's email. This is not the standard—and those policies can have both positive and negative ramifications.

Several years ago, we met an entrepreneur from Russia who was visiting Silicon Valley. What we didn't understand during our first meeting with him was the reason for the visit. While his ability to communicate in English was impeccable, he was unwilling to open up to us about the details of his company. It was impossible to get a direct answer from him about some very basic questions, including how the company was funded, when they would run out of cash, how decisions were made, and what roles each of the founders played in the company. Our overall impression was that he was being uncooperative, at best, or trying to hide the true status of the company. His style did not fit Silicon Valley and we suspect he was unsuccessful in raising capital in the Valley.

A phenomenon that began in Silicon Valley is the *stealth mode* company. Startups in stealth mode do not disclose what the company is doing, who has invested in the company, or who works there. Sometimes this is done for legitimate competitive reasons. We suspect other times it's being done to create intrigue and convey the notion of being *cool*.

Savvy entrepreneurs figure out how to provide the appropriate level of information and candor to maintain their credibility without jeopardizing truly confidential information. So remember, openness and transparency are a part of the culture of Silicon Valley—and what's required if you're going to do business here.

- **Boil the Ocean** – The most successful companies we've seen are tightly focused on a particular customer set; have an easy-to-explain and easy-to-implement revenue model; and adopt a direct, efficient go-to-market strategy. One of the biggest challenges we see with entrepreneurs is their attempt to do everything, a.k.a., boiling the ocean. Going after too many different kinds of customers, pursuing a convoluted business/revenue model, and chasing ambitious plans at the same time—all are recipes for failure. Take small steps, test, and iterate. Then move to the next phase.

What Was Old Is Now New Again

The VC comic ran from 1997 to 2000 and is still relevant today

- **Pieces Fit Together** – In the best businesses, all the pieces fit together. It's about the right product for the right customer, coupled with the appropriate business model and an efficient, cost-effective distribution and customer support strategy. Too often, we find that companies have built their businesses piecemeal only to find that those pieces of their business don't fit together. For example, the pricing doesn't make economic sense, or the business model does not get the company to profitability in an appropriate time frame.

We worked with a Colombian-based company that was building a business focused on the Latin American market. Because of some family connections, the founders were able to secure a few customers in the United Kingdom. But the U.K. customers weren't useful as reference customers in Latin America, and the revenue generated from the U.K. customers was minimal. What's more, the company also wanted to launch into the U.S., which was very different from the Latin America (LATAM) markets. The company had a small team with limited resources, and focusing on proactively developing these new markets would mean allocating limited staff and capital for travel. We suggested they nix the U.S. and U.K. expansions and remain focused on strengthening their position in LATAM.

- **Good Enough** – A Silicon Valley best practice is to get a product into the market as soon as is practical. This means develop a good-enough product—also known as a "minimum viable product" (MVP)—and ship it! By good enough, we mean a product that meets approximately 80 percent of the customers' prioritized needs and requirements. A crucial error many companies make is waiting until the product is *perfect* before shipping it. Companies that make this error often spend months building a product without any customer input, only to find out it isn't what the customer wanted nor what they are willing to buy.

  In addition to supporting the development of an MVP, it's important to get feedback from customers early on in the process. What's their impression? Does the product fill a need? Will it work for their business? Will they pay for it? And if so, how much?

- **Company Scaling** – Successful Silicon Valley companies know how to scale and to develop significant market share. They have figured out how to cost-effectively reach their customers with a product or service those customers will buy.

  We met a pair of founders with a good business idea, but they had an ineffective and inefficient approach for reaching their targeted customers, which were restaurants in Mexico City. Initially, the founders served as the sales team, calling on restaurant owners and managers to secure orders one by one. As they grew, they hired additional salespeople in their target market. But with more than 10,000 restaurants in their target market, they had to find better, faster, and cheaper ways to sell. The founders could have looked for other companies calling on the same decision makers at restaurants, but they did not. One of the reasons they failed was that they continued to sell directly instead of finding partners, making strategic alliances, and developing cross-promotion opportunities.

- **Go Big or Go Home** – Most of the companies in the Valley leverage some element of technology in their businesses. The ecosystem here is designed to help those companies grow revenues to hundreds of millions of dollars, and also to find a path to liquidity through public offerings or sales of the companies. Because of this, companies have to identify big market opportunities and develop go-to-market strategies that allow them to quickly gain significant market share.

In many other regions some companies are not based on technology and are not looking to grow to billions of dollars in revenues. In fact, we work with many companies that have no- or low-tech operations, and we really enjoy working with them. They are often a breath of fresh air—good companies run by savvy entrepreneurs who are pursuing more mainstream, but definitely solid, market opportunities. While these businesses are typically not appropriate for Silicon Valley markets or funding, they can benefit from the best practices developed in Silicon Valley.

- **Global Mindset** – Visitors to Silicon Valley have often commented that many of the companies based here are known throughout the world, despite the fact that some are not very large or prominent. Silicon Valley companies understand that creating a larger-than-life perception often adds value. Companies create this in several ways. For example, if your website is in multiple languages and accepts multiple currencies, people will perceive your company to be doing business on a global basis, regardless of the reality.

> *Today, you must have a global perspective to compete with everyone else.*
>
> – Kayvan Baramound, SV101 Ventures

When you first establish your business, you should think about whether the company has global potential—otherwise you may be forced into being a global company before you're ready by competitors from large, well-financed international companies. We met a startup in Colombia doing a great job of building a business there. However, the founders had to accelerate the company's internationalization plans for LATAM—specifically Mexico—due to the impending launch of a competing Spanish multinational into Mexico.

On a strategic and operational level, you have to be prepared for the fact you may have to operate globally before you're really ready. All too often we hear entrepreneurs say, "We have no competition except Google and Facebook, and they are not here...yet." If your market is interesting and attractive, other multinationals will be there sooner than you want.

- **Pattern Recognition** – The use of pattern recognition helps founders understand customer and market opportunities, sales objections, and other business issues. The most adept founders we've met are expert at spotting patterns in their business and using that information to effectively target customers and manage their sales process. Often these patterns emerge as a result of questions such as "Are there more customers that look just like this one?" or "Why does this sales objection keep coming up?" or "We seem to be attracting interest and inquiries in a very different market from the one we are focused on. Do we really understand what's going on?"

Gathering information about customers and markets is a continuing process. It's good to do it before you build the product, but it must continue to be done on an ongoing basis. The question that arises regularly during market feedback and analysis is this: How much data is enough to make a decision? The answer is that you don't need thousands or even hundreds of data points, nor should you rely on a single customer's input before you make a decision. Good pattern recognition requires collecting data points until the trends, patterns, or clusters become obvious. When discussing patterns, we are very fond of saying, "One is a dot, two is a line, and three is a trend." However, to validate a trend, you need more than three and less than one hundred.

We met a team of Brazilian entrepreneurs building a business that provides tutoring services to high school students. They discovered that most of the sales inquiries and customers were actually working professionals who were seeking tutors. These professionals needed help in passing professional certification tests to make them eligible for job promotions and career advancement. The Brazilian team recognized that the real need for their service was very different from their original vision and target market. Given how wrong many entrepreneurs are in identifying the correct initial market for their product, it is important to collect data and to be biased by what the data tells you.

- **Failed Experiments** – Silicon Valley provides the opportunity to experiment. Even though companies are formed with certain ideas around product and market, the reality is that until they find a successful product/market fit, they remain in experimentation mode. That mode, which can last for months or years, is something that nearly every company goes through. As Eric Ries describes in his book *The Lean Startup*, one of the best practices in the Valley is to build a "lite" product, test it, and, if it's the wrong product, change it. Ditto for the market.

So companies in the Valley experiment until they succeed, until they run out of money, or until key members of the team leave. Failures come in many sizes and forms—ranging from building the wrong product to colossally misjudging the timing of a launch. Webvan is an example of poor timing. The company spent over $1 billion to prove what most people at the time already knew—that a trip to the grocery store wasn't a pain point for enough people at the time. Pets.com filed for bankruptcy less than one year after going public, in part because its customers determined that paying to ship fifty pounds of dog food across the country when it could be bought locally didn't make sense; and, given the financial markets at that time, the company couldn't raise the additional capital necessary to get to the break-even point.

"Every startup has a license to experiment."

– Martin Pichinson

Martin Pichinson

Marty Pichinson is CEO of agencyIP, a company that licenses technology for both large and small companies. He is also the founder and co-CEO of Sherwood Partners, a leading firm that handles the shutdown of failed venture-backed companies. Pichinson and his organization have closed down more than 300 companies.

"There are many reasons why companies fail. For one thing, most founders make poor CEOs. A founder should be Chief Concept Officer, not CEO. It's true that Mark Zuckerberg is both, as was Steve Jobs, but they are anomalies.

"In the Valley, every entrepreneur has permission to experiment, but not to fail. Hopefully, a company will find enough people to embrace what it's doing before it runs out of money. And fear of failure is often what makes people move quickly enough to make this happen. But remember: The odds are totally against you."

- **Perseverance and Perspective** – It can take a long time to build a startup into a large company, in part because the period of experimentation takes time before the company hits its stride. Consider Instagram, for example. Founded in 2009 and launched in October 2010, Instagram was acquired by Facebook for over $1 billion in 2012. The popular press continues to state that the acquisition was only eighteen months after the 2010 launch date, rather than the actual 2009 founding date. This adds to a skewed perception of how long it takes to build and scale a company. Kevin Systrom, one of the

Instagram cofounders, has stated, "Instagram is an app that took only eight weeks to build and ship, but was a product of over a year of work." One of our quirks, as humans, is to assume that the first time we hear of a company marks the beginning of that company. That misperception causes most of us to believe that startups achieve success much faster than is actually the case.

Every venture capitalist would be happy with an Instagram-like return in such a short time frame. However, venture investors know that most of their investments will take five, seven, or as much as ten years from company startup to liquidity. As Biz Stone, a founder of Twitter, says, "Timing, perseverance, and ten years of trying will eventually make you look like an overnight success."

- **Storytelling** – Good communication is an essential part of the founder/CEO role. Most entrepreneurs are not naturally good presenters. Effective presenters need to be good storytellers and determine the best ways to engage with their audiences. Whether presenting to investors, customers, and potential hires, or when networking at an event, it's extremely important that you gauge the situation (audience and attention span) both before and during your presentation. Being effective means that you understand what's of interest to your audience and know your content cold. Good presenters are effective at telling an engaging story in a simple, uncomplicated manner with a crisp and clear message.

Learning how to be a good presenter takes practice, and then more practice, until it feels comfortable and natural. Faith in you, as an entrepreneur, comes from how you carry yourself and how you present your ideas. Ultimately, what matters is the quality of the business idea and people's confidence in your ability to execute on that idea.

We've seen hundreds of entrepreneurs imprisoned by their slide decks. PowerPoint or Prezi can be your best friend or your worst enemy. A great presenter is a great storyteller who engages the audience. A bad presenter narrates the slides and exudes no confidence. A slide deck should be used to reinforce or enhance the story, not to *be* the story. Steve Jobs once said, "People who know what they're talking about don't need PowerPoint."

In general, the quality of presentations in Silicon Valley is actually very high. For those outside the region, attending pitch competitions and demo days is an excellent opportunity to see how entrepreneurs present their ideas, and to see the difference between mediocre, good, and great presentations.

• **Selling** – While many founders believe that building product is their single greatest contribution to the company's success, we politely disagree. The product does have to work; it's hard, if not impossible, to sell a mediocre product. But in almost every case, *selling* is the most important aspect of building a business. Selling matters right from the beginning. The founder is the salesperson who inspires cofounders and team members to join the company. Founders also meet with initial customers to close deals. And at every step in the process, the entrepreneur is selling his or her vision of the company as they bring on investors, employees, and others who will support the company's growth.

Since Silicon Valley thrives, in part, on connections made by *random, happy accidents*, becoming good at communicating and selling is helpful because you never know whom you're going to meet, or where you'll meet them. You may be provided with a new customer simply by sitting next to someone at lunch. Silicon Valley is a place of serendipity, particularly for those who are prepared.

• **Value Trumps Features and Function** – It's natural when talking about your product to discuss its features and functions. However, Silicon Valley customers and investors know that it's the value of the product, not its features and functions that counts. Early adopters are not dazzled by technology; they are more concerned about whether a solution can provide them with real economic and business value.

Entrepreneurs who want to sell to these early adopters have learned the importance of clearly communicating the impact of their product on the customer's business. Some examples of value include: how the product increases the customer's bottom line or installed base, and how the product saves the customer time or makes it easier to do business. Experienced entrepreneurs ask lots of questions of customers, partners, and market experts as they craft a clear and concise value message. And they modify the value proposition as they uncover new information and insight about how the product impacts the customer. Understanding and communicating value is an integral part of market development and sales process.

- **Pay It Forward** – Silicon Valley has built a powerful "give and get" community of entrepreneurs. We encourage entrepreneurs with whom we work to do what Silicon Valley has done, and continues to do: Pay it forward and help one another. Helping fellow entrepreneurs can come back to you in the form of new contacts, prospective customers, and new ideas. So if you're the recipient of help, remember to appropriately recognize and reward those who help you. There is no free lunch.

Yahoo! offices in San Francisco

- **Something That Matters** – Today, we face big problems in the world, problems that cry out for solutions. Many of these are problems where technology could make a difference—from water conservation to mapping deforestation, tracing illicit drug distribution channels, bringing the unbanked and underbanked online, and reducing human trafficking and slavery. We know of a startup in Brazil that uses geolocation technology, government satellite imagery, and the distinctive chemical signature of illicit drugs to identify the location of temporary drug manufacturing sites. They then alert local law enforcement agents, who shut down the facilities.

  Of course, there are many significant social problems around the world, and it is great to see an increasing number of entrepreneurs addressing them. These problems are worth solving. The challenge is to create viable, successful, and sustainable businesses that become part of the solution.

- **It's Complicated** – While we would all like to believe that the path to success is a straight line, reality does not support this belief. In the world of startups, twists and turns, complications, and unexpected challenges always arise. These include raising capital, identifying and closing customers, and meeting milestones. Everything takes longer than you expect and is fraught with challenges. The reality is: You work like crazy, you stumble and fall backward, you fail numerous times, and perhaps then you make a bit of progress. So be flexible and nimble as you navigate through your business dealings. Hang on. Your fifteen minutes of fame are coming!

- **Luck and Serendipity** – Entrepreneurs want to believe they are going to be successful based on the quality of their product, their team, and their uniquely identified business opportunity. And certainly these attributes do contribute to success. But often success is based on being at the right place at the right time, and fulfilling the needs of a customer or fitting into a company's acquisition strategy. While hard work and great products are important, luck and serendipity can have far more impact on a company's success than anything else.

> *"I attribute a ton of our success to luck. Everyone who's successful has been lucky. They've also been able to recognize opportunities and take action, but most of their success is still based on luck."*
>
> – Phil Libin

Phil Libin

Phil Libin is cofounder and executive chairman of Evernote and a venture partner at General Catalyst Partners.

"Evernote was created when we combined two teams in 2007. We had been working in California on a project that would give everyone a photographic memory, and I had a team in Boston that was just leaving a startup. They wanted to do the same, so we joined up. There were lots of benefits to that plan, but it also added a lot of complexity to the structure of the company, which made us pretty much unfundable by any Silicon Valley investors.

"We initially made it work by putting our own money into the company and getting angel funds. Then we found an investor in Europe. It took us about six months to clean up our structure. On the day we finally finished, the market collapsed. The investor called us and said he was pulling out because his fund had lost most of its value in that one day. So I decided that I was going to shut the company down before we completely ran out of money. I went to bed thinking that in the morning I would go in and lay everyone off. Right before I went to bed, I got an email from some random guy in Switzerland saying he really liked the product, that it had made him really organized, and had changed his life. He also asked if we needed any investment. I emailed him back and said something like, 'Yeah, we could use some investment.' And twenty minutes later, we were on a Skype call. I explained the situation and he said he could help. A few weeks later, he wired us half a million dollars. That was enough to keep us going, and we started doing better. We were able to get six more months of traction.

"There's a lot to be said for being in the right place at the right time, opening yourself up for more and better quality opportunities, anticipating good fortune, and having a bit of luck. So to improve your chances of unexpected good fortune and serendipity, open your mind, connect with lots of people, change your routine, rebound from learning experiences, and be willing to take risks."

- **Learn from Failure** – Keep in mind that Silicon Valley is filled with more failed companies than successful ones. It's important to recognize that experimentation, and often failure, are part of the process. What's important to remember is that failure offers the opportunity to learn from mistakes. It takes courage, or the mastery of fear, to manage through the challenges of a startup when things begin to stall. Serial entrepreneurs have figured out how to handle adversity, rather than letting adversity handle them. It's therefore no surprise that some investors will invest only in experienced entrepreneurs.

  Unexpected things will occur, deals will go south, contracts won't get signed, budgets will get cut, employees will quit, and a whole host of other things might happen. We spend a lot of time with startups, mentors, and investors helping them understand what can wrong, so that they can plan ahead, develop contingency plans, and navigate through the challenges. When setbacks occur, the most successful entrepreneurs confront the issues head on, identify alternatives and contingencies, and make what are often difficult decisions to keep moving. While it's okay to be afraid, and it's okay to pause, inaction is not an option. Getting help from fellow entrepreneurs, mentors, and advisors can provide you with perspective during challenging times.

- **Enjoy the Journey** – The journey of a startup is like no other. It's full of highs and lows, positives and negatives, and it's unlike anything else you ever experienced. You'll be confronted with situations and problems constantly, and you'll learn to do new things every day. If you see this as an exciting challenge rather than a daunting problem, and if you decide to go through this process, then you've got to love it. And if you love it, you're more likely to be good at it.

Once you've gone through this experience, you will look back and be amazed at what you did, what you said, and how you handled difficult situations. Sometimes it will seem surreal, like a scripted scene from a movie. We encourage you to write down your impressions and experiences as you go through the process, since your memory is fallible and your recollection and perspective will surely change. Enjoy the journey.

CHAPTER 6
Breaking the Rules...and Other Tactics

More often than not, being an entrepreneur means that you may need to break rules. Those rules can be as simple as challenging conventional wisdom and range all the way up to testing the limits of the law without breaking it. The challenges inherent in building a business often require entrepreneurs to find creative ways around rules and constraints.

Mark White of the law firm White Summers Caffee & James says, "The simple truth is that Silicon Valley historically has had nowhere else to look to for guidance and inspiration. We embrace breaking existing rules and making up new ones as needed. Typically, the rest of the startup world looks at what works here, and then imitates it."

Many of the venture capital firms in the Valley not only like rule breakers, but actively seek them out, since disrupting existing industries is often the key to building a large, successful business and generating outsized investment returns.

We know many entrepreneurs outside Silicon Valley find it difficult to break the rules. In lots of places, entrepreneurs *do* follow the rules and conform to local traditions, behaviors, and customs. That's not the way we do things here.

The most fundamental rule that entrepreneurs frequently break has to do with the status quo. Too often people believe that if a problem is worth fixing, someone would have already fixed it by now. But successful entrepreneurs don't accept that thinking. They identify problems, find creative ways to solve them, and build innovative products and companies to successfully address market opportunities. Sometimes those opportunities are in underserved markets, while at other times they address entirely new markets. Today, hailing a taxi seems archaic. We wonder why someone didn't think of Uber sooner.

Uber, the company transforming the taxi industry today, is a good example of what we mean here. Historically, companies providing transportation needed their drivers to carry a special license permitting them to operate in the local municipality. Uber considers its service "on-demand transportation," and treats its drivers as independent contractors, rather than as employees (a status that may not endure). The rule that Uber has "broken" is the one that requires drivers to carry a livery license. And as a result, Uber vehicles are not regulated as traditional taxis. Today, Uber has more than 327,000 active drivers who set their own schedules and offer transportation on demand. The app is available in 300 cities and 60 countries (2015 Uber data).

Salesforce.com, Inc., is another company that has broken the rules. Before that company was founded, the generally accepted "rule" was that you couldn't sell software to large enterprises without a direct sales force. And you certainly couldn't sell software as a service (SaaS). But CEO Marc Benioff left Oracle, a successful enterprise software company, and proved that he *could sell software via the Internet*. Today Salesforce.com has numerous Fortune 500 companies as customers, and the company's annual revenues in 2015 were $5.37 billion.

AirBnB is yet another company that has broken rules. In most municipalities, homeowners are prohibited from renting all or part of their homes for less than 30 days. Today, many municipalities are changing their rules to accommodate AirBnB, and some cities are also requiring payment of a hotel occupancy tax on short-term rentals. Across the world, AirBnB has more than 2 million listings, and the company recently expanded its offerings to include homes in Cuba.

Finally, there's Elon Musk—a habitual rule-breaker. He has repeatedly done what others thought was impossible. Specifically, he has built a successful electric car company, and he has created a company to compete with NASA in providing space shuttle services. He has even broken the rules in small ways—developing an electric vehicle, albeit expensive, that can go from San Francisco to Los Angeles on a single charge, something previously deemed unfeasible. And he's testing a space rocket that is reusable.

So ask yourself: Where would companies like Uber, Salesforce.com, and Tesla be if they had followed the rules? They needed to think different, to break away from conventional wisdom, to do things that ran contrary to the "rules." And sometimes their rule-breaking has fallen into legal gray zones. However, keep in mind that there are *rules for breaking the rules*. You cannot do things that are patently illegal such as stealing a car (there's no gray zone there!); and you should not do things that are immoral. Neither should you do things that call into question your credibility or your integrity. But that still leaves a lot of room to maneuver and to defy what everybody thinks is the "right" way to do things.

All of these are examples of what we call strategic rule-breaking, in which the status quo is questioned, laws and regulations are challenged, and opportunities are created for transforming industries. Other kinds of rules can and should be broken—rules we would label "operational." Here's an example.

Salesforce.com's lobby sign

"Random isn't always random." – Selcuk Atli

Selcuk Atli

Selcuk Atli is a serial entrepreneur and the cofounder of the venture-backed companies Socialwire and Boostable. Combined, the two companies have raised approximately $10 million in capital.

Selcuk Atli grew up in Turkey and came to the U.S. as a Fulbright scholar. "When I arrived in Silicon Valley in April 2011," he says, "I didn't have a job and didn't know anyone here. I wanted to meet someone who could mentor me, but I found that most events were overfilled with people looking to meet people. So I found a better way.

"I wanted to meet Bing Gordon, former Chief Creative Officer at Electronic Arts, a board member at Amazon, and a partner at Kleiner Perkins. As I was looking for investment in my first company, I attended a conference where LinkedIn founder Reid Hoffman had been scheduled to speak. However, Hoffman couldn't attend, so Gordon was scheduled to speak instead. I asked the conference organizers if I could talk with Gordon, but they said no.

"I knew that right after Gordon's talk, lots of other folks would be crowding in to talk to him. I also knew there would be little value in a short, shake-your-hand conversation. So I devised a plan. The conference hall had two exit doors. Figuring I'd rather have a 50/50 chance of a real conversation than a 100 percent chance of a handshake (which had a probability of 0.5 percent of any real follow-up), I positioned himself near one of the two doors. I was lucky—Gordon left through the door I had chosen. I introduced myself and briefly explained why he should meet with me. When Gordon explained that he was headed out on vacation the following day and didn't have time to meet, I offered to drive him to the airport. Gordon agreed. I then connected with Gordon on LinkedIn so that he would know I was legitimate.

"Despite his tight schedule, Gordon asked his assistant to schedule a meeting with me prior to his departure. I did not see the assistant's email until 10:30 that night, as I was on a date. The email suggested a breakfast meeting at 6:30 a.m. the next morning at the Rosewood Hotel, and requested that I send a copy of my slide deck about the company. Despite the fact that I sent the slides close to midnight, Gordon had reviewed them prior to the breakfast meeting. I later met with a number of KP partners. Ultimately we both concluded that Socialwire was too early in its development for a KP investment. However, I gained a great contact and mentor. Later, Gordon was instrumental in introducing me to a number of people at Amazon, which helped me with early customer traction."

Selcuk broke an operational rule—the one that says you wait in line to talk to a speaker after a speech. But he did not break the law—that is, he did not follow the VC home and "ambush" him there, which might have gotten him arrested for stalking. This is a great example of what we mean when we recommend breaking "operational rules." For many startups it's the small rule breaking that can make the difference between getting a meeting with an investor or customer—or not. Being courteous, professional, *and* persistent will often get you what you want.

Finally, let us remind you that there is a fine line between being persistent and recognizing when a no means no. We cannot give you much guidance on this topic other than to say that having a good intuitive sense is part of being a successful entrepreneur. The Silicon Valley mindset is that rules are meant to be broken. Asking for forgiveness, not permission, is the norm here, and it really works!

> *"Real entrepreneurs are persistent."* – John Scull

John Scull

John Scull is a venture capitalist at Southern Cross Ventures.

"The characteristics of real entrepreneurs? They believe in what they're doing, they're committed to success, and they're super-smart. This allows them to attract talented people to join them. The difference between good entrepreneurs and great ones? Resilience—and the ability to learn from their failures. For these, the only issue is whether they are focused on a market problem that's big enough, with customers in real pain.

"Sometime after an initial *no* from an investor, an entrepreneur wants to go back to see that investor again. If you're just presenting the same information, don't bother. But if you've made progress, then it's okay—since your persistence is rooted in progress.

"When people in other regions of the world get introduced but receive no reply, they assume that the other person is not interested. But in the Valley, you need to keep pursuing people, to be doggedly determined. Here, life is Darwinian; it is survival of the fittest."

Additional Characteristics of a Great Entrepreneur

Silicon Valley entrepreneurs are resourceful, find the shortest path to get things accomplished, and always assume that a competitor is right behind them. They are obsessed by success, not consumed by a fear of failure. The most successful entrepreneurs are focused on execution and always drive toward success. What fuels their hard work and long hours is not the money. Rather, it's the desire to make a significant impact on the world. Questioning the status quo, identifying new technologies that solve problems, and creating new businesses for changing markets are all powerful motivators.

Many additional traits are common to successful entrepreneurs—among them passion, commitment, open-mindedness, and self-awareness.

Beyond these general characteristics, Silicon Valley entrepreneurs possess a range of skills that make them highly effective. Let's take a look at some of them.

- **The entrepreneur as problem-solver** – Entrepreneurs in the Valley have a spirit of self-sufficiency, plus a desire and a willingness to problem solve when no one else can or will. By definition, most startup founders are engaged in solving problems that have not been solved before. They are resourceful and high energy; and ideally, they understand when they're out of their depth and need to call in outside help. Their job is simultaneously all-consuming, exhausting, and exhilarating.

  In many regions of the world, we find that people look to the government to fix things, or wait for someone else to put solutions in place. More worrisome, we sometimes find that entrepreneurs assume the same attitude when it comes to their own startups. Often these entrepreneurs believe that programs offered through an incubator or accelerator will magically solve the problem of figuring out their business plan, finding their customers, and raising capital. Programs in incubators or accelerators can help, but it requires a committed CEO to take the lead in figuring out what's needed and in moving the company forward.

> *You need to know what you don't know. If you lack sufficient humility, people can't save you from yourself."* – Joe Kennedy

Joe Kennedy

Joe Kennedy led the turnaround of the failed startup that later became Pandora. The music sharing site went public in 2011 at a valuation of over $3 billion. He is currently chairman emeritus of the company.

"The original Pandora was founded in 1999. When I joined, there were thirty people working at the company without pay. My wife didn't understand why I would want to join a company that was emblematic of failure, but I saw people with a passion for purpose; it was what I looked for in a startup. The team's attitude was to believe 100 percent in what they were doing.

"The vast majority of the time, we ran with that full conviction, though we would occasionally take stock of where we were. I see young, smart entrepreneurs who restrategize their company every Monday. Their presumption is that if something is hard, the strategy behind it must be wrong. But every success I've ever had has been really hard. In the early days the needle doesn't move at all...and then one day it moves a little.

"I ascribe the success of Pandora to a team that was *focused*. How does a little company ever win against larger companies? The answer is focus, combined with passion and purpose. In a small startup, everyone is focused on one thing. In a big company, people are focused on many things. We didn't look for more to do; frequently we looked for *less to do*.

"Having the best product or service today is more important than developing the right brand or finding the right channel to market. The Internet allows people to find the best products and services in the world for their needs. If you cannot be the best in the world, do something else.

"What does it take to be a great entrepreneur-leader? You need both chutzpah and humility. Most people get the chutzpah part. But the humility part is critical. It takes humility to recognize that you don't have all the answers, that you need people different from yourself to make a success. You need to know what you don't know. If you lack sufficient humility, people can't save you from yourself."

- **The entrepreneur as risk-taker** – In Silicon Valley, most entrepreneurs recognize that what they are doing is risky. But only the truly experienced entrepreneurs recognize just how risky their path truly is. Smart entrepreneurs do everything possible to lower the risk as they build product, get customer traction, and make key business decisions. But it's also important to remember that in Silicon Valley you are expected to take risks—and it is okay to fail. That's part of the reason so many entrepreneurs migrate to this area.

In 2009, we met a young entrepreneur in Armenia who was not yet old enough to rent a car. When he announced his intention to become an entrepreneur, he defied his family's expectations about his career. Further, he told us that if his startup failed, he would have to leave Armenia because he would shame his mother and his mother's family, and also his father and his father's family. The stakes were clearly high, and his family's tolerance for failure was very low. In the end, he took the risk and succeeded in building a company that employed dozens of people.

Intel in Santa Clara

"They are not judging me for my past, but for who I might become in the future." – Beverly Parenti

Beverly Parenti

Beverly Parenti is the founder of The Last Mile, a nonprofit technology accelerator that prepares incarcerated individuals for successful reentry through business, entrepreneurship, and technology training.

"The United States contains 5 percent of the world's population and 25 percent of the world's incarcerated individuals. The U.S. prison population has increased by 700 percent since the 1970s, and the rate of recidivism in California is 67 percent.

"The mission of The Last Mile is to provide on-site education and marketable skills to prison populations so that individuals have the ability to get a job when they are released. We believe that getting a job is the key to successful reentry. Without a job, the men don't have self-worth—and they are a drain on society. Our hope is to help break that cycle by getting individuals ready to move into an internship program in a company.

"Through our in-prison program, the men learn about entrepreneurship—how businesses function, how to work with a team, how to accept feedback. They gain confidence in their abilities both to grasp new ideas and to pitch ideas; and they learn to pivot when they are headed down the wrong path. With the help of volunteer mentors, guest speakers, and leaders from the business community, the men are introduced to the latest technologies, though *without access to the Internet* or any hands-on experience.

"Mentorship provides many benefits for the men. They say to themselves, 'Here I am behind bars, inside a facility with barbed wire and gates. And here is someone from the real world—a certain caliber of person—who is taking time to talk with me as a human being, not as a prisoner.' That's really powerful. They are so thrilled that people care enough to come into the prison. The mentors offer really sound advice, and the participants soak it up.

"I often hear the men say, 'They are not judging me for the crime I committed, like the prison administration does. They offer an almost unconditional acceptance of me as a person. They are not judging me for my past, but for who I might become in the future.' "

- **The entrepreneur as jack-of-all-trades** – Entrepreneurs must do everything. There are a number key factors that we believe increase a Silicon Valley entrepreneur's chances of success—finding a cofounder who possesses a complementary background, and building a core team that has prior startup experience. When we refer to *complementary background*, we mean complementary domain, work experience, personality, and skill set.

Not everyone can or should be an entrepreneur, despite what a few "startup experts" claim. Some people have personalities or other characteristics that make them poor founders or CEOs. Very often a company founder needs a cofounder who complements or supplements his or her talents.

The entrepreneur also assumes the important role of chief team-builder. Teams matter. Building the right team—one that can work well together and execute on the vision—is critical to the growth and success of the startup. There are simply no successful one-person companies. Great leaders need to build great teams in order to build great companies.

There's one last aspect unique to Silicon Valley: The entrepreneur here serves in many roles, often being hands-on as chief product officer, chief salesperson, and chief fundraiser. This multifaceted operational role is very different from the "general manager" role prevalent at companies in other regions. We know an Australian startup CEO who left the critical business decisions around U.S. product opportunities and an initial target market to a third-party distributor who was brought on board to "figure out how to generate sales." This hands-off approach runs contrary to the way things are done here in Silicon Valley and is not well-received by investors, should the company want to raise capital here. One of the many reasons that companies are successful in Silicon Valley is that there is tremendous interaction with the customer that leads to products better suited to customer needs and identifying follow-on product opportunities.

- **The entrepreneur as experimenter** – Silicon Valley entrepreneurs will try different things until they find the right combination of product, market, distribution channel, and business model that yields success. So what does experimentation really mean? It could mean changing the product and its functionality, the market it serves, or the messaging and pricing. Since solutions are typically not obvious, entrepreneurs take their best guesses—and when those don't work, they evaluate options and try something else.

> *The highs were higher and the lows lower than I had ever experienced. An important lesson was that when something didn't work, you dusted yourself off and started over again. In the job of startup CEO, you have twenty things to do, ten that have to get done—and you can only do two.*
>
> – Zia Yusuf, BCG Consulting

While many late-stage investors are not interested in waiting until these elements of the business are sorted out, some early-stage investors and angels are willing to throw money at a team with an interesting concept. They recognize that the business model will become clearer through trial and error. These investors are more likely to fund an A-quality team with a B- or C-quality idea, rather than a C-quality team with an A-quality idea. For them, the quality of the management team is critical to figuring out a business that can succeed.

During the process of experimentation, market feedback sometimes indicates that the initial product or market targeted is wrong. In such cases, it's necessary to "pivot." Startup investor and advisor Chris Yeh defines pivoting as making substantial changes to your business plan *before* you've built the final product and gone to market. He also believes that if you've already gone to market and find that you need to dramatically change the fundamentals of your business, you'll be doing a company *restart*, not a *pivot*. Experimenting, risk-taking, and pivoting as necessary are integral parts of finding a formula for success, and are Silicon Valley best practices that can be applied to companies elsewhere.

Tesla showroom in Palo Alto

"Pivot or reboot?" – Chris Yeh

Chris Yeh

Chris Yeh is an angel investor and VP of marketing at PBWorks.

"People talk about pivoting, but most have not read the books of Steve Blank or Eric Ries. Actually, pivoting does not mean raising $20 million and spending it on the market, only to discover your concept is wrong and you need to start over. It means testing a hypothesis *early*.

"We also use the term 'pivot' too often when we really mean 'reboot.' Reboots of businesses are happening more frequently these days because companies are getting funded without the appropriate level of market development beforehand. Instead of determining the right product/market fit, companies are raising money and abdicating any responsibility or judgment. If a company must reboot, why not just return the money to investors, and let them decide if they want to reinvest in the new concept?"

Tips from the Trenches

As an entrepreneur, it's not only your character traits that matter. It's what you do on a regular basis. Here are some tips on how successful entrepreneurs think and act, drawn from our work with entrepreneurs throughout the world.

- **Socialize the Idea** – Successful entrepreneurs find that by socializing their ideas with others *in person*, they get feedback on how to improve those ideas. Specifically, they get competitive information, they build networks of contacts and relationships, and they are often pointed toward advisors and customers who can help transform their ideas into viable businesses. So talk it out.

“ The best thing about Silicon Valley is how much access there is to mentorship. It starts with people in the company, then the board, investors, mentors, friends and other professional connections. Many are more accomplished than I am. I don't think I have ever had a problem finding someone to meet up with here. ”

– Phil Libin, Evernote and General Catalyst

- **Listen to Everyone but Follow No One** – In the process of socializing your idea, you will gain a lot of input. But ultimately, you—the entrepreneur—have to figure out the best way forward. Talking to many people and occasionally (perhaps frequently) getting shot down helps you identify key issues and concerns. It also helps you gain perspective on what makes sense for your company, and how to address issues that may hinder its success. Often there are no obvious answers. Your job is to sort through conflicting feedback and decide what to do next. It's your company—and the market will determine whether you're right or wrong. Everything else is just opinion.

- **Engage Your Supporters** – Entrepreneurs need supporters both inside the company and outside. Team members with prior startup experience can be invaluable assets to the company. They've learned by doing, they understand what they're in for, and they have experience that helps them maintain perspective. Supporters outside the company—mentors and advisors—can also be quite helpful, especially when they provide candid feedback and (when appropriate) tough love.

It's important to find people who think differently because it forces *you* to think differently. A Danish entrepreneur recently told us, "If I want to talk to myself all day, I will find people [advisors and board members] just like me. But I don't. So I won't."

As a founder, you will experience lots of challenges, many of which can be discussed with your team. However, there are other issues that you, as founder and CEO, will find inappropriate to discuss with either your team or your board members. These might include how you handle personnel matters, or how you deal with your own limitations and uncertainties. In such situations, outside advisors can be most valuable. You need to find people whom you trust, who will listen with compassion and empathy, and who will provide helpful, unbiased input.

- **Cultivate Diversity** – When we talk of diversity, we are often talking about age, religion, country of origin, sexual orientation, economic standing, or education. One of the hallmarks of the U.S. in general, and of Silicon Valley specifically, is that the people who live and work here come from all over the world. Nearly half the population in Silicon Valley was born outside the U.S., and more than 100 languages and dialects are spoken here. This is in stark contrast to many other regions of the world where there is vastly more homogeneity and conformity. Diversity in work experience, domain expertise, skill set, and ways of approaching a problem are equally important within your company.

  Recent data on workforce diversity reveals that companies whose founders actively encourage diversity show increased productivity, higher levels of creativity and innovation, and a more entrepreneurial approach to problem solving. And companies with more diverse teams are more adaptable and responsive to market needs.

  We have worked with a number of startup teams that paid little attention to diversity. In one particular company, they approached key business issues from a singular perspective and with a closed mindset. The team was unwilling to seek out or accept other perspectives. The result was that they ignored product and market options that could have provided significant business upside and growth opportunities for the company.

  If you want to build a more successful company with better products and a stronger leadership team, look for *different*, not *same*. Cultivate all kinds of diversity in your company and surround yourself with people who come from varying backgrounds, cultures, and experiences. Diversity continues to contribute to the richness of Silicon Valley.

- **Focus on Execution, as It's Everything** – There are lots of smart people and great ideas in Silicon Valley. In fact, most of us have had the experience of seeing a new product or service and thinking, *Hey, I had that same idea a few years ago!* The good news is that you have identified a good idea. The bad news is that you *didn't do* anything about it. Ideas by themselves have zero value. An idea is simply a starting point for experimenting until you find the *right idea and product* around which you can build a business. The value of an idea lies in the tangible steps you take to build a product that works, and to validate a market for that product.

For many entrepreneurs, building the product consumes a significant amount of their time and attention. However, the product is only the first step in building a business. Finding a market, validating it, identifying customers, and closing sales take significant time, energy, and effort—frequently, more than what was required to build your initial product. As it turns out, this is really hard stuff to do.

> **❝** *You have to ignore the obstacles in order to focus on where you want your company to be. If there's something in the road you don't want to hit, you don't look at it— you look past it. You have to look to the place you want to be, not the place you don't want to be.* **❞**
>
> – Phil Libin, Evernote and General Catalyst

Being a startup founder is all-consuming, and it's easy to get diverted and lose perspective. This is one of the reasons we encourage founders to find trusted advisors and mentors who ask good questions, provide objective feedback, and help maintain your perspective. Don't drink your own Kool-Aid.

> *"The hot breath of competition is a positive thing."*
>
> – Ann Winblad

Ann Winblad

Ann Winblad is cofounder and managing general partner at Hummer Winblad Venture Partners, a pioneering venture capital firm founded in 1989.

"Hummer Winblad has passed on a number of successful startups. We flog ourselves annually for our sins of omission—those deals we should have invested in that turned out to be big winners. But it's always hard to know if the outcome would have been the same with a different group of investors. There is a magical dynamic that occurs between the investor syndicate and the entrepreneur; the choices you help the entrepreneur make early in building the management team *do* make a difference. Who knows? With us as investors, they may not have been a grand success.

"Net Manage was a company that we passed on. We loved the CEO: During our meeting, he kept getting orders for the product over the telephone. But we were worried about the competition. So we called a number of companies—and we found that Microsoft had twenty people working on the same product, Sun had thirty, and IBM had fifty. But if we were to play that movie again, we might have noticed that those three companies were putting tons of resources on developing a product—but they didn't have anything yet. Meanwhile this guy is selling his product like hotcakes.

"Our lesson is that you will always find big guys toiling away at stuff that entrepreneurs do better. That's in part because, once the entrepreneur figures out the product, he doesn't just drop it off at the customer's office and say, 'We are done,' which is what Microsoft, Oracle, and IBM do. The entrepreneur continues to nurture the customer and develop the product. As an entrepreneur, you are always ahead of the market. And if you cannot feel your competitors breathing down your neck, you're not in a good market in the first place. The hot breath of competition is a positive thing."

- **Learn to Say No** – For most startups, the hardest thing to do is to say *no* to a customer or an investor. But in a number of instances, this is the right response.

When your product is designed for a large market with many potential customers across geographic areas and industries, potential opportunities will surface that are outside your current plans. Most of these opportunities will not fit your near-term plans, and you should say no. In the early stages of building your business, it's critical that you remain focused, disciplined, and selective in pursuing your initial target customer.

But, having said that, we should acknowledge that regions with smaller markets sometimes force entrepreneurs to be more opportunistic—and to take whatever business is available, since the number of customers in any given market segment may be limited.

Here's another instance when *no* is the right answer: We have seen companies try to do two things at once. We know of a company where half of the employees were developing software products while the other half were engaged in contract development for other firms. Individually, each business could have been successful, but together in one organization the situation was challenging at best. Conflicts arose in priorities, allocation of resources, and differing management skills required to run each business.

Plug and Play Tech Center in Sunnyvale

"Saying no is difficult." – Danilo Leao

Danilo Leao

Danilo Leao is the founder CEO of BovControl a Brazilian company providing innovative solutions for the cattle industry.

"After a couple of visits to Silicon Valley, I have learned a great deal about Silicon Valley's best practices. For example, I learned to say no.

"When is saying no difficult? Every day I feel the pressure. I don't want to lose an opportunity, but if it's not aligned with my strategy, I won't do it. I met a customer who wanted my company to customize our product for him—a project that was not on the roadmap for the next two quarters. I said no. I was also offered a round of investment by a venture capital firm that was more money than our company was looking for. If I took it, there would be too much dilution of equity. Again I said no—and took less money from another investor."

- **Get Comfortable with Uncertainty** – When you are building a startup, there's a lot of uncertainly—and often more questions than answers arise. It's very difficult to predict where a startup will be in three months, much less three years. You need to develop a vision and a plan for what the company will achieve, recognizing that what you project three years out will likely change over time. While your projections most likely will be inaccurate, there is value to the discipline of building a plan, developing underlying assumptions, and setting key metrics and milestones for the business. It is easier to hit a target that you can actually visualize. Experienced entrepreneurs understand that the initial business concept and plan are just the starting point; ultimately, the business will change, often in unpredictable ways.

Given the lack of clarity about the future, entrepreneurs need to adapt to the fact that they will never have enough information to make fully informed decisions. We met a Brazilian founder who was constantly investigating, researching, and developing different business scenarios for his company. The problem was that he never had sufficient information—nor would he ever gather enough within the required time frame to make a decision. And his inability to make a decision put the company in a perpetual holding pattern.

Things happen, and things change. It's nearly impossible to predict the future with any degree of certainty. However, once you accept that the startup journey is uncertain, it's easier to make decisions and move forward. Feeling comfortable with not knowing everything is just part of being an entrepreneur.

Why Alignment Matters

Alignment is a crucial area that can mean the difference between success and failure for a startup. It's also a topic entrepreneurs don't spend enough time thinking about as they build their company. When we talk about alignment, we mean both alignment within the company—between the founders and core team—and alignment outside the company—with customers, partners, and investors. Silicon Valley is acutely aware of where misalignment frequently occurs. Here are eight key areas to watch for.

- **Vision** – Alignment begins with vision. The vision of a company needs to be clear and well thought through, and every member of the team needs to be in alignment with that vision. It is the foundation on which the company will build its product, go to market, raise capital, and achieve success.

  Recently, we came across a startup team in Brazil with a great product and market opportunity. However, two of the three founders wanted to build a sustainable business, while the third wanted a "quick flip." Sorting through these issues splintered the team and took valuable time away from the market validation process. In the end, "Mr. Quick Flip" left the company. Clearly, the founders were not initially aligned around the company's vision. Their motivations and their vision for the end game were quite disparate—a situation that defocused and distracted the team and nearly cost them their opportunity in a promising new market.

- **Product/Market Fit** – Most startups struggle with product/market fit—because it's excruciatingly hard to nail down, even in Silicon Valley. Aligning a product with a market means finding a customer who needs the product now, is willing to pay money for it today, and is willing to buy from an unknown startup with a limited or nonexistent track record. Finding this fit is usually a process of iteration and experimentation. Here's how that process should work:

  - **Step 1 - Identify:** Most startups begin by identifying a problem and creating a premise for a product that could serve as a potential solution in the overall market. Ideally you have talked to enough people to validate that this is an important problem with large market potential.

  - **Step 2 - Create and Validate:** Typically, a startup team builds a *lite* version of the product. Then, as quickly as is practical, the CEO goes out and talks to companies that the team thinks would be ideal initial customers. This process takes time, with numerous conversations often required to identify the right product/market fit. Teams with a well-thought-out theory of who the customer should be typically get their answers to the product/market fit question sooner. On the other hand, startups that believe *everyone* is their customer often struggle to identify who really cares enough to buy the product.

  - **Step 3 - Review and Assess:** The team uses market feedback to refine the product, or to redefine the initial target customer. Then they go back to the market to see if they can close a sale.

  - **Step 4 - Listen and Identify Patterns:** If the target customers don't buy, the team spends time listening to their objections and identifying recurring patterns as to why that particular market may not be a good fit. When they find they are selling the right product to the wrong customer, they go back to step 3.

In a perfect world, you get the process right the first time. In the real world, however, steps 3 and 4 often require a lot of iteration. It's better to complete the experimentation and iteration processes early. By figuring out the fit, it makes it easier to raise capital—and at a higher valuation.

We have also found that having appropriate domain expertise on your team often gets you more quickly to the right product/market fit. Today's businesses and enterprise customers are more knowledgeable than ever. They often take a proactive role in identifying technologies and products that will solve their problems and meet their needs. To take advantage of such knowledgeable and sophisticated potential customers, you have to build the right product—and for that you need to have domain expertise on your team.

- **Commitment** – Building a startup is hard work. The process requires long hours, flexibility in the face of inevitable twists and turns, and self-sufficiency. Founder, cofounders, and team members all must be aligned in their commitment to the company. Does this mean that you put other parts of your life on hold? Probably.

> **❝** *No one ever said that entrepreneurs can have all the things in life and can still start a company.* **❞**
>
> – Chris Yeh, PBWorks

We have seen entrepreneurs attempt to work on several companies at once. Jack Dorsey is one example. He's the CEO of the troubled public company Twitter, and now the CEO of Square, a public company. Such an arrangement rarely works out well for both companies. Lack of 100 percent commitment on the part of any team member is one of the key reasons that startups fail.

As an entrepreneur, you need to be willing to get your hands dirty, and to recognize that no one will do the work for you. While there are a lot of available resources—incubator, accelerators, mentors, and advisors—*you* are ultimately responsible for making things happen in your business. For example, while someone can make introductions for you, the only way to build your network is by attending events and conferences yourself. It works the same way in the sales process. You need to be effective in building a pipeline, selling product, closing sales, and supporting customers. No one will do these things for you. (For a review of the underlying process for building and curating your network, see Chapter 3.)

Raising capital is a long, arduous, and sometimes convoluted process even for Silicon Valley companies. You may be able to get an introduction to an investor, or you may meet one at a conference or networking event. But finding the right partner at the right venture capital firm in order to close a round of financing requires an amazing amount of time, energy, fortitude, and good luck. While you must take the lead in the financing process, the entire team needs to be working in support of this goal at the same time that they are building the business.

> *We have the smartest people in the world working harder than anyone else. Look at the partners at Sequoia Capital. These guys work 6 to 7 days a week, 12 to 15 hours a day, every day of the week.*
>
> – Derek Andersen, Startup Grind

- **Roles and Responsibilities** – Success depends on ensuring that the right people with the right skills are in the right positions in your company. Determining this alignment—who is responsible for what—is an extremely important task, both during the initial phase and as the company grows and scales up. We often see misalignment among founders in their roles and responsibilities, which causes problems in building the business and in raising capital. And remember, the amount of stock each person holds in the company has nothing to do with roles and responsibilities.

Be thoughtful about the mix of skills, experience, and domain expertise necessary for your company to be successful. Where are the holes in your team? Can you get the expertise from contractors, mentors, and advisors, or do you need to bring in another founder so you can amass the requisite skills? Can the current team work together effectively? Being clear about roles and responsibilities early helps to set the tone and culture of the company in the future.

> *It's easy for a CEO to get trapped in the role of Chief Technology Officer (CTO), overseeing product development and engineering because the product is never finished. You need to put the same energy and resources into developing user engagement, marketing, and selling. The startup changes, and the CEO needs to change, to adapt, and to be flexible.*
>
> – Balazs Farago, Real5D

We worked with a first-time CEO some years ago who did not understand that the CEO's role is to run the business, while the board of directors' role is to provide oversight and suggestions. The CEO took the board's suggestions as directives, which ultimately created turmoil among both board members and the management team. Instead, when the CEO met with the board, he should have said, "I appreciate your input and suggestions, and I will get back to you with my decision."

"Make sure they are the right people." – Rachel Faller

Rachel Faller

Rachel Faller is founder and creative director of Tonlé Design, a zero-waste, fair-trade fashion label in Phnom Penh, Cambodia.

Rachel Faller had a vision for creating a zero-waste fashion label in Cambodia with clothing and accessories made primarily from recycled materials. Today that vision is a reality. Her entire production process leaves no waste compared to a typical clothing factory, which can average up to 40 percent waste.

While Faller is now the sole founder at Tonlé Design, she originally had other partners in the company. She describes a number of areas where misalignment created problems as she was trying to build her company. The lessons learned during this experience remain relevant as her company continues to grow.

"When I was looking for the right people to bring onto the team, I wanted to find partners who cared about the women I worked with. I was more concerned about the social side of the business than I was about the numbers or making sure that the partnership made good business sense.

"Proper business due diligence on partners, even if the company is more about a social cause, is critically important. What's more, I learned that getting to know someone both in a work context and outside of work, and perhaps working with them on a project in advance, is probably a good idea. I could have assessed the working dynamics before going into a partnership.

"And if you're dealing with someone who is coming into your company as a cofounder or board member—someone who is getting equity, but who has not necessarily contributed money—it's really important to have a vesting period. You need to understand the real value of someone who is investing their time or intangible resources. Make sure the equity distribution properly reflects that value.

"At the time I went into the partnership, I was personally overwhelmed. I was stressed, my judgment was clouded, I needed helped, and I was burnt out. Never make deals when you're backed into a corner or feel at your worst. You won't make good decisions because the other person has the upper hand. You never want to make a deal when you're in that position.

"I would like to have a cofounder on the ground in Cambodia, but after going through different partnership scenarios, I want to make sure he or she is the right person."

- **Decision Making** – Making decisions is not a process of consensus. Nor is it based on the stock ownership of the individual members of the team. There must be clarity among the team as to how decisions get made, and recognition that the final decision rests with the CEO, who is ultimately accountable. Once this alignment has been established, how the decision-making process works and what input comes from the team are up to company management to sort out.

  Finally, decision making needs to be done in a timely manner. While most people want to wait until they have gathered complete information before making decisions, waiting is a luxury most startups can ill afford.

- **Timing** – Making decisions in a timely manner, and communicating them clearly throughout the company, are key practices in building alignment among your team. In thinking about timing, there are three important questions to ask yourself: Are decisions being made in a timely manner? When is the right time to take action? How long will it take? We've seen entrepreneurs paralyzed, unable, or unwilling to make decisions, while they waited for more or better information. This can severely undermine morale.

  When is the right time to take action—to expand into a new market, or to hire new employees? You build alignment by understanding, acknowledging, and carefully considering any underlying issues before making a decision. Then you make your decision, and clearly communicate it to the team.

Investors look for entrepreneurs who understand the importance of timing. They often want to know how long it will take to build the product, to get the customer, and ultimately to achieve liquidity through the sale of the company or a public offering.

Additionally, it's essential that you make sure the team is committed for the length of time it takes. Nothing hurts the startup's credibility more than when a key member of the team leaves after two years because he or she has lost interest. Investors don't look kindly on that. If the company founder leaves to join another company or starts something new, potential investors may even pass on the new company. As large as Silicon Valley is, it is still a very small place—and investors have long memories.

- **Exit Strategy** – While the exact outcome and timing of a company's liquidity event are functions of circumstance, both the management team and the investors must be aligned on how much capital the company will raise, how the company is going to build out its organization, and when a liquidity event will most likely occur. In reality, this plan gets updated regularly, based on current market conditions, competitive environment, and the company's ongoing success.

John Scull of Southern Cross Venture Partners points out the importance of clarity around timing when talking to investors. If investors expect a company to get to liquidity in three to four years, that's fine—unless it actually takes double that time. Even among angel investors who tend to have a shorter investment time frame, Scull has seen instances where angels have been 'patient money', waiting for a return in five to seven years *if* that time frame was part of the original plan.

Most entrepreneurs we meet start companies so they can make an impact. However, the practical reality is that both investors and the management team want the company to find a path to liquidity at some point—either as an IPO or more frequently via acquisition.

We've met a lot of entrepreneurs who haven't developed a realistic path to liquidity. They have little idea who might want to acquire them, or how best to position the company to maximize its value. Investors are always entering a deal with their exit strategy in mind. Entrepreneurs need to do likewise.

- **Work Style and Culture** – Every company has its own unique work style and culture. While there is no right culture, the culture of your organization needs to align with your values and your operating style; and more important, it needs to fit with the values of your target customer base. So if you're selling a product to CFOs, you may want to build a culture that focuses on financial metrics; whereas if you're selling the product to HR professionals, you might be better served by developing a culture that emphasizes a collaborative sales approach. The demeanor, personality, and communication style of your team need to be aligned with your target market, as well.

Why Companies Fail

Silicon Valley is known for its successes, not its failures. However, understanding the causes of startup failure can help you as an entrepreneur avoid them. In Silicon Valley, we do talk openly about how failure is part—and sometimes, the final outcome—of experimentation. No one, either inside or outside the Valley, really knows how many companies have failed versus those that have succeeded. Do we simply have more successful companies because we have more failed ones? What is our success rate compared to other regions?

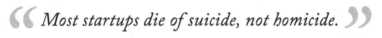

Most startups die of suicide, not homicide.

— www.insight.vc

Plenty of statistics exist on the number of companies receiving angel or venture financing, and the amount of money invested in each. And individual venture capital firms have data on failed companies in their own portfolios. But no one has complete data on the number of companies that are started each year, nor on the number that go out of business. So we are left guessing as to how well Silicon Valley really does. It is fair to say that of the companies that do succeed, many are more successful than companies in other regions of the world. And even that generalization is undermined by the success of international companies such as China's Alibaba and Tencent.

While most venture investors will admit that not every company they invest in is successful, they are frequently complicit in downplaying failures. Companies that have gone out of business are often removed from the list of investments on the VC's website. Often, when a company is sold for less than the capital invested or for no return on investment, the investors will state that the company "was sold," implying that it was a successful investment. Entrepreneurs sometimes play the same game. "Our company was sold for $100 million" may sound like a great win for the founder. But if the investors have preferences that guarantee them the first $90 to $100 million because of the liquidation terms of their stock, those investors get essentially all the proceeds of the sale, while the entrepreneur and management team are shut out of any meaningful financial gain.

So why do companies fail? The simple answer is that they have run out of money, and whatever they were doing didn't work. Or it worked, but not as successfully or as fast as expected. Or the company needed more investment capital than it could raise. To understand Silicon Valley and the startup ecosystem, it is important to delve into some of the underlying reasons that startups fail.

Analysts at CB Insights (www.cbinsights.com) tracked and reported on over 100 startups that failed. Not surprisingly, they found that only a few failed in building product. Most failed due to poor product/market fit, or to issues among the founding team. See the table on page 122 that illustrates the top reasons companies fail.

Here are several noteworthy conclusions from the CB Insights reports:

- The actual death of a startup is often hard to pinpoint, since many companies limp along for years in zombie-like fashion without any significant market traction.

- We tend to fawn over the billion-dollar exits and hear little of the failures. In the blog A Smart Bear (http://blog.asmartbear.com), Jason Cohen notes, "The fact that you are only learning from success is a deeper problem than you imagine."

- In every year since 2010, some 70 percent of all startup deaths have been in the Internet sector.

- The mobile sector has seen far more volatility and far more than its share of dead companies.

- Mobile talent is highly coveted and has historically made mobile-product firms prime targets for "acqui-hires." In an acqui-hire, a company is purchased strictly for the expertise of the employees working there, rather than for the startup's products or customer base.

- Many companies raise significant amounts of financing before failing. In fact, the average amount raised by companies before failure is $11.3 million.

And here's a summary of the reasons why companies fail, as self-reported in blogs, tweets, and articles by those closest to these companies. The list provides some important insights.

- Founder issues: founder misalignment and disagreements

- Product/market fit: not something people wanted, wrong approach, or wrong target market

- Timing: premature scaling or too early for the market

- Go-to-market issues: didn't solve for distribution

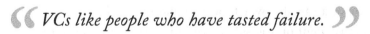 *VCs like people who have tasted failure.*

– Martin Pichinson, agencyIP

Top 20 Reasons Startups Fail: 101 Startup Post-Mortems

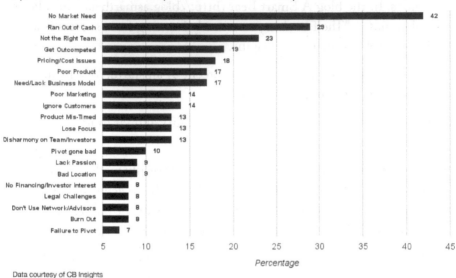

Data courtesy of CB Insights

What makes Silicon Valley fundamentally unique is the attitude toward failure that those who work here hold. Specifically, it is the *company* that fails—not the *individual*. We understand that many of the reasons for failure lie outside the control of the entrepreneur. So unless the entrepreneur did something really stupid (and that does happen!), the startup community looks at the failure as a failed experiment, not that the individual is flawed and has failed. Even the laws in the United States support this notion. When a company goes through bankruptcy, neither the investors nor the founders are held responsible for the debts incurred by the company. Risk and failure are an integral part of the experimentation process in building startups; you cannot have success without both of them.

In Silicon Valley, we don't fixate on failure; we focus on success. While we look at failure as a valuable way to learn what not to do, there is no real time and energy spent on the subject of failure or ways one can fail. Most important, the possibility of failure does not dissuade us from trying to build success—and that's one of Silicon Valley's best-kept secrets.

CHAPTER 7

"Silly Valley"

They tell us never to underestimate the savvy of entrepreneurs. So we won't. While we think there's lots of great information in this chapter, you probably already understand Silicon Valley. You have managed to avoid the hype, and you have a good sense of what's real and what isn't, right? Let's see. Here's a short quiz you can use to test your own savvy. Score greater than 90 percent (the bar here is awfully high) and you can skip right over this chapter. Score less? Read on.

Quiz: True or False

1. It is easy to be successful in Silicon Valley.
2. Warm introductions guarantee you a "deal."
3. It is easy to raise money in Silicon Valley.
4. The U.S. market is large, homogeneous, and easy to access.
5. Our startup has no competitors.
6. Venture capitalists are infallible gods.
7. Silicon Valley is always right.
8. Success begets success.
9. The path to success is a straight line.
10. A perfect pitch is all you need.
11. Everything sells for a billion dollars—or more.
12. It is not Silicon Valley, it's "Silly Valley"—and dumb things happen here.

Answers: All are false except #12. More than one wrong answer, read on. Perfect score, skip this chapter and work on your business!

What we have found is this: The further away from Silicon Valley you are, the more your view of the Valley is shaped by misinformation, along with stories and anecdotes that don't necessarily reflect what's really going on here. Specifically, there's a naïve view that the region is filled with nothing but successful startups, all of which receive venture capital financing. Below we deconstruct the most common misconceptions so that you can develop a more accurate picture of what is real and what is fantasy.

1. It is easy to be successful in Silicon Valley.

It is, perhaps, easier to be successful in Silicon Valley than in other parts of the world. But for every successful startup here, there are hundreds—if not thousands—that fail, and many more that struggle to gain customer traction.

Visibility within a given sector, momentum, revenue growth, market share, and profitability are all used to measure success. Some entrepreneurs define success as having built a company that has become a household name, regardless of whether it makes money or even has significant revenue. Others believe that having one million users is in itself valuable. We disagree. If there is no way to monetize the attention of those million users, then they are of questionable value.

Startups selling in Silicon Valley and the U.S. are challenged by the complex nature of the sales process here, the cynical mindset of customers, and a highly competitive environment. The sales process at large companies can be very complex, with many senior managers involved in making purchase decisions. Moreover, customers can be skeptical about the claims that startups make about their product performance. While a new product may actually be fifty times faster than or cheaper than the customer's current product, startups will often gain more credibility by claiming only five times improvement—since that may be more believable, and sufficient to close the sale.

Very often we hear the following from entrepreneurs outside the Valley: "If I'm so brilliant and my product is so cool, why isn't everyone buying it?" The answer is simple: Frequently the product isn't as compelling as the market needs—or as competitive as products from the ten, twenty, or thirty other startups competing in the same space. Also, while U.S. customers are willing to buy from companies that are not local, those startups need to provide the requisite level of service and support—something that can challenge nonlocal companies.

2. Warm introductions guarantee you a "deal."

Silicon Valley is a meritocracy. You are ultimately judged on the quality of the product and its fit with the customer's needs. While an introduction can be valuable, a customer's buying decision will be based primarily on the severity of their problem and ability of the product to deliver real value. So while relationships and introductions are important, you should consider them merely starting points to closing a contract.

The same principles of meritocracy and fit apply when raising capital. So while lawyers or mentors can introduce startups to investors, the investment decision is rarely, if ever, based on the source of the introduction.

So when you want to acquire customers or raise capital, you cannot and should not depend on these insiders' networks alone. *No one* can possibly know all the right people. What's more, lawyers or mentors will only make an introduction when they think it is warranted.

> *If I don't think an investor will invest, I won't introduce the entrepreneur.*
>
> – Derek Andersen, Startup Grind

3. It is easy to raise money in Silicon Valley.

There is a naïve perception that Silicon Valley is a region filled with nothing but startups whose founders have successfully raised venture capital financing, and that any startup that raises venture capital will be successful. The reality is that of the thousands of companies in Silicon Valley, very few actually do raise venture capital. Consider the following data point: In 2013 fewer than 350 companies raised initial Series A financing from venture capitalists. This represents a very small fraction of the companies looking for capital in the Valley. (We do acknowledge that many startups raise capital from friends, family, and angel investors, and these are not reflected in the data point above.)

Among the companies that do raise capital from VCs, there's no assurance of a company's success. In a typical venture capital portfolio, investors generally expect one or two out of every fifteen companies to be successful. (Success here is defined as returns that are ten or more times greater than the original investment.) Investors will lose *all* their money in at least half the companies in their portfolio, and they'll be lucky to get between ten cents and a couple of dollars back for each dollar invested in the rest.

Most entrepreneurs don't recognize that the vast majority of venture capital in Silicon Valley is invested in growth companies that have achieved some momentum in the marketplace, not in early-stage startups. Today, those companies include such names as Dropbox, Box, Uber, Lyft, and AirBnB.

Raising money isn't easy. And raising money from angel investors is sometimes more difficult than raising money from traditional VCs. That's because many angel investors are investing their personal money in what for them may be a risky, single investment—not part of a portfolio of investments. Angels are typically reluctant to lead a round of investing, which often involves setting a price per share for the company stock and taking a board position; most angels prefer that traditional venture investors assume these roles. Despite these factors, angels do serve as a source of capital for startups, often backing entrepreneurs who are in their extended networks.

While some U.S. venture investors can and do invest in non-Silicon Valley and non-U.S. companies, most VCs prefer companies with management teams in Silicon Valley who are—at least initially—selling into the U.S. market. A handful of venture capital firms that *have* dedicated funds for international investment often require that one or more of the startup's management team spend time in Silicon Valley. There are exceptions. But coming from outside the U.S. makes it more difficult for a company to raise capital here.

4. The U.S. market is large, homogeneous, and easy to access.

For many startups, the United States represents a very large market opportunity compared to markets elsewhere in the world. In the U.S.—and in Silicon Valley, in particular—many customers are willing to buy from startups.

While it's true that the U.S. offers the advantage of a single currency and language, it is in fact a very challenging market for most startups. There are 25 to 30 major metropolitan markets; and the style of doing business in San Francisco is very different from that of New York City, which is different from Dallas. Also, in the U.S. market, startups face the challenge of lots of direct competition, as well as knowledgeable and sophisticated buyers who are actively looking for the best product and demanding high-quality service and support. Being successful requires that a company be adequately financed, with a rollout plan that is thoughtful, appropriately timed, and properly staffed.

Misconceptions abound relative to the distance between Silicon Valley and other parts of the United States. For example, some people are surprised to find that it takes an entire day (check-in and time zone changes included) to fly from San Francisco to New York or Boston. And while a place like Denver may be part of the western United States, it is not close to Silicon Valley. In fact, it is about the same as the distance between Belfast, Northern Ireland, and Rome, Italy. No one in their right mind would headquarter their company in Rome if their primary market was in Belfast.

Many entrepreneurs who envision selling directly to U.S. customers find doing so quite challenging, due to the cost and complexity of building direct sales and support teams. This scenario often leads startups to pursue a sales-agent relationship. Rarely is this option a good choice. We find most manufacturers' reps to be third-tier bit players who lack both the geographic reach and the financial capacity to build a big business, particularly in the tech sector.

Many startups are interested in partnering with large companies to build sales and market share. But too often, startups are not ready to engage in these types of discussions. Four key criteria determine a startup's readiness to partner with large companies. First, the product has to be sufficiently developed, tested, and validated so there is no question regarding whether it works as promised. Second, the product's value proposition must be clearly articulated to the market for which it is targeted. Third, the startup must have a clearly defined customer profile, and must know how to sell to that customer based on direct experience. (Obviously the target customer needs to be one that the potential partner can successfully reach.) And finally, the large company must be able to dedicate significant money and people to the partnership. The good news is that many large companies are both interested and committed. The bad news is that a startup team can be overwhelmed by the demands placed on it by the larger company, especially when the latter's team is bigger than the entire startup team.

We met the CEO of a Singapore-based startup who was interested in working with a large systems integrator such as IBM or PWC to sell product to large enterprises. The problem was that the startup team had no idea who their target customers were and had no experience selling to large enterprises. By engaging with a partner, the startup expected that the large firm would do that work for them. However, that's not what a partner does well. A large partner needs the startup to have identified and sold to the target market *before* the partnership is formed. A large partner can often make valuable introductions, provide credibility, and help in the sales process, but it cannot do the initial selling or identifying the right customer. That is a process that the startup needs to do.

For startups wanting to partner with large U.S. corporations with local subsidiaries in the startup's own region, it is important to form an initial relationship with the local subsidiary, and use that subsidiary as your advocate at headquarters. Some large U.S. companies will not talk to a startup about partnering or investing until that process has occurred.

5. Our startup has no competitors.

For entrepreneurs who plan to operate businesses in their own regions, an understanding of the local competitive landscape may be enough, because large global players are not active in your market—yet. However, for companies looking to expand globally (including into the U.S.), a thorough analysis and understanding of your global competition is necessary—and frequently overlooked. How do we know this? The symptoms of inadequate competitive analysis manifest in the following ways:

- Failure to identify both *direct* competitors and, more important, *indirect* competitors—those that provide a different approach to solving the customer's problem.

- Underestimating the ability of large, global companies to enter a startup's region. Today many B2C companies have no borders—witness: SnapChat, Facebook, and Twitter.

- Tendency to focus solely on product features and functions in analyzing the competition. One of the ways to differentiate your company from the competition and to build more value for your business is to look beyond your product and product features. We have seen companies achieve success by focusing on key vertical markets and developing a deep understanding of customers' needs and pain points. These companies went on to build market share, visibility, and significant presence in those vertical segments. And in doing so, they created a defensible barrier to competitors.

6. Venture capitalists are infallible gods.

Many venture capitalists are smart and well connected, true, but that does not make them right all the time. They are willing to take risks, understanding that only a small number of their investments will be successful. But they also know that among those success stories, a few will return a VC's initial investment many times over.

Venture capital investment alone does not guarantee a company's success. Likewise, the lack of venture investment does not mean that the company won't or can't succeed. Many companies have succeeded without early-stage venture investment—among them, Braintree, GitHub, Atlassian and Mail Chimp. And many VCs have missed out on backing some very successful companies.

"I still read that email just to kick myself a little bit."

– David Lee

David Lee

David Lee is a venture partner at SK Telecom and cofounder of KStartup, an early-stage accelerator located in Seoul, Korea. He is also a limited partner in both Y Combinator and Silicon Valley Angels.

"One of the deals I passed on was with a guy I knew from another deal. His new idea was one he had been working on because his girlfriend was very into fashion and clothing, but he had no retail or fashion experience. It was an app called Tote. I asked for a business plan. He sent me an outline of the idea, a Word document with a few photos. I didn't really go for it, but I was polite and kind of kept him interested. He didn't have a cofounder at the time, so there was an opportunity for me to work with him more closely. However, I sort of ignored him. But he was very persistent...email after email. Another year passed and finally he went for the 'hard close,' saying that he had found a cofounder and was going to close a small round of funding at a valuation at $1.5 million. I declined the deal and wished him well. His name was Ben Silverman. Later, while still on his email chains, I saw that he had changed the name of the company to...Pinterest. I still read that email just to kick myself a little bit."

Not only did I turn down Uber twice, but I turned down Lyft as well, either of which could have been my best investment of all time

— Dave McClure, 500 Startups

We encourage you to look at the Bessemer Ventures website, where you can see a long list of companies the firm decided not to invest in (see Appendix A). This list proves that even smart investors sometimes pass on good investment deals.

What Was Old Is Now New Again

The VC comic ran from 1997 to 2000 and is still relevant today

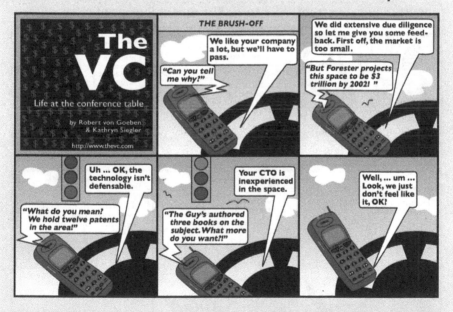

7. Silicon Valley is always right.

Just because Silicon Valley embraces a new idea or technology, or investors invest, it doesn't mean that the idea or technology will be successful. Webvan is a great example. In the late 1990s, Webvan raised over $1 billion in an effort to change the grocery business. Investors believed that by providing a fully integrated delivery service, Webvan could change consumer behavior. Turns out they were wrong. The model that Webvan adopted—building its own stores and distribution centers—was not cost-effective at the time. Today, fifteen years later, a number of companies—including Google, Amazon, and Instacart—are gaining traction in the grocery home-delivery business.

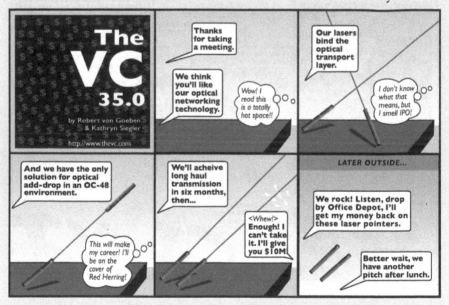

© Robert von Goeben and Kathryn Siegler. All rights reserved. More at www.thevc.com

Many other examples come to mind. While everything in the Valley today seems to be about mobile, social, and SaaS, there are still a number of companies selling good old-fashioned, server-based enterprise software—even though many consider this kind of product a dinosaur. People outside Silicon Valley don't recognize that what seems like an emerging trend may turn out to be another failed experiment. Just because we're experimenting with something doesn't mean it's going to work. And just because it's fashionable doesn't necessarily mean it is right.

"The downside of Silicon Valley is its herd mentality."

– Joe Kennedy

Joe Kennedy

Joe Kennedy led the turnaround of the failed startup that later became Pandora. The music sharing site went public in 2011 at a valuation of over $3 billion. He is currently chairman emeritus of the company.

"Silicon Valley is very parsimonious with money before a startup has demonstrated traction. You can raise a little bit of money to explore, but you need to run pretty lean. However, once you've demonstrated traction, there's plenty of capital to grow your business.

"The problem with big companies is that they anoint a winner before traction has been demonstrated, or they are too parsimonious with their funding—and nothing gets a chance to succeed.

"The downside of Silicon Valley is its herd mentality. To a degree, it's irrational. When the investment climate is good, Silicon Valley invests a lot, but in tough times the Valley doesn't invest enough. The time it takes to reach liquidity is often disconnected from the business cycle."

8. Success begets success.

Just because somebody works at [*pick a company name*], it doesn't mean that person has been instrumental in the success of that company. Nor does it mean that the person's style is necessarily going to result in success if he or she joins another company. Hiring experienced people is valuable to a startup, but hiring the *right* experienced person is more likely to result in success. Make sure that every member of your senior management team has the right background, experience, skill set, temperament, and contacts to add value to your company.

Some of the most successful CEOs are not the founders of their companies. Remember Tesla, that well-respected automobile manufacturer? CEO Elon Musk is often described as its "brilliant founder," having founded PayPal, SpaceX and several other companies. But in fact, the company was founded in July 2003 by Martin Eberhard and Marc Tarpenning. It was their vision to create an electric car with both speed and efficiency. Musk came to the company as the day-to-day, operational CEO in October 2008. He transformed the company's initial vision into an automotive manufacturer producing hundreds of highly innovative vehicles every week. Sometimes founders create success, sometimes it's their *replacement* who does.

9. The path to success is a straight line.

Too many entrepreneurs believe that the path to success in Silicon Valley is a straight line. It isn't. Many successful companies here have changed course along the way. They've had a change in management, a change in product, a change in the target market—or all three. And, having made these changes, some companies still fail. Assuming that everything will work as planned is both unrealistic and unsupported by the data.

> *You can be a smart failure here and still be employed.*
>
> – Bill Grosso, Scientific Revenues

Entrepreneurs new to the Valley often infer that it's easy to build a company because those who have achieved success unintentionally abbreviate the story of how long the process took them from idea to outcome. Along the way, some of the pertinent details are omitted. Moreover, many entrepreneurs are inexperienced at running a startup, and therefore are overly optimistic—which can make them poorly prepared to navigate through the starts and stops, and twists and turns, that a startup experiences. Thinking about contingency plans and alternatives requires a discipline that often does not come naturally to the inexperienced.

10. A perfect pitch is all you need.

A pitch is an important part of a startup's plan—especially for hiring employees, acquiring customers, and raising capital. But it is a minuscule part of the overall process of building a business. Investors and customers make commitments based not on a slick PowerPoint presentation, but rather on the credibility and track record of the founder/CEO and management team.

We have seen numerous startups proudly showcase the awards they've won in business-plan or pitch competitions. But in Silicon Valley, business traction counts far more than winning an award. While it's important to be able to succinctly describe your business on paper or in a pitch, it's more important to be able to execute on your plan. Customer revenues are the true measure of success—not the number of awards and prizes won.

11. Everything sells for a billion dollars—or more.

Stories. Tall tales. Lies. Call them what you wish. Silicon Valley is full of them. Everything *doesn't* sell for $1 billion. It's the exception rather than the rule. It's true that Oculus sold for $2 billion, WhatsApp for $19 billion, and Nest for $32 billion. And it's true that Tumblr and Pinterest's acquisition prices were equally impressive.

Yet those are outliers. The educational software company Kno—which raised nearly $100 million in venture financing from blue chip investors, including Intel Capital, Andreessen Horowitz, Silicon Valley Bank, and

Silicon Valley Angels/Ron Conway—sold to Intel for a reported $15 million. Investing a dollar and getting back fifteen cents was not a very good return for those venture investors. The reality is that most venture-backed companies fail, sometimes closing or being sold for ten cents for every dollar invested. Enjoy the stories. And don't take them too seriously. Focus on building value in your company.

12. It is not Silicon Valley. It's "Silly Valley"—and dumb things happen here.

Dumb things happen here. That is why our nickname for Silicon Valley is Silly Valley. Don't get us wrong—Silicon Valley is a great place. But inexplicable, stupid, and absurd things do happen here, just as they do everywhere else in the world. Companies get funded or acquired that shouldn't. A startup loses a sale to a competing product that doesn't do the job. Companies get acquired for $1 billion when there's no there, there. HP acquires another company for billions of dollars—only to shut it down a year or two later.

We've seen it all: flaws, warts, and the challenges that startups face when they come to Silicon Valley. Some companies with great products cannot get any traction with customers or investors, while other companies, for reasons unknown, find a ready and willing audience. Sometimes we can predict this ahead of time, sometimes not. But regardless of the outcome, we still encourage entrepreneurs to work with trusted Valley-based people who can help you get beyond the hype, who can tell you when you are getting into "Silly Valley territory."

We recently attended the Demo Day presentations at a well-known Silicon Valley incubator. Forty companies presented to several hundred well-connected executives and angel investors. Other than the pedigree of being associated with a prestigious incubator, we found very few startups that were investment-worthy. Most were not venture-type deals. (Sorry, but a catering business is not a venture deal.) And many lacked any competitive advantage or unique technology. We just shook our heads, recognizing that while this was early 2015, it might just as well have been the year 2000. If it makes no sense, why are others investing? They probably don't know any more than you do. The lesson here? It doesn't make sense because…*it doesn't make sense*. Have another glass of Kool-Aid.

What Was Old Is Now New Again

The VC comic ran from 1997 to 2000 and is still relevant today

CHAPTER
8 The Road to Silicon Valley

Sooner or later most entrepreneurs visit Silicon Valley. They come to see how the Valley works, to understand why entrepreneurship flourishes, and to find ways to leverage and apply that insight to their business. Silicon Valley is a laboratory for entrepreneurs, a place where everyone experiments with the process of building and scaling a company. Entrepreneurs here are honored and valued in a supportive environment. In this regard, Silicon Valley is unique—and definitely worth experiencing firsthand.

But when companies arrive in Silicon Valley from outside the area to raise capital, this is too often what we hear:

- "I've built a cool product."
- "I've sold it to a few customers, people I know."
- "I'm running out of money."
- "I'm in Silicon Valley because I've heard it's easy to raise money here."
- "My slide deck has 35 slides with no financial projections, and is the same one I use with investors at home."

Because we work with so many startup founders from around the world, we are usually the first ones to tell them that the above approaches to raising capital are not going to work in Silicon Valley. Here's why:

- **Partial story** – U.S. investors want a 360° view of your business in the *first meeting*. This requires a 10- to 15-slide presentation that can be delivered in 20 minutes or less. And it must provide a clear, concise overview of all elements of your business. This is different from the norm in other regions of the world. A number of Brazilian startups we've worked with have told us that local venture investors don't want to see the company's financials until the third or fourth meeting.

- **Little or no vision** – Too many companies fail to present a big vision. They can't articulate why they are game changers, or how they will disrupt an industry or capitalize on a global market opportunity. Their presentations provide too much data and lack the requisite insights to support a compelling story about their business. They don't present information in a clear, logical way, one that persuades investors that the team and company can execute on a plan and the vision.

- **Vision is not credible** – When companies do articulate a big vision, it is often too big. One founder we know claimed that his company's vision was to become the next Facebook. Like so many others, this founder failed to present credible underpinnings for his vision: Specifically, he lacked a roadmap of how he would achieve this goal in a step-by-step manner.

- **Good, but not great, product** – While a good product may get you customers in your own region and perhaps some in Silicon Valley, investors and customers are much more interested in a great product. A great product provides significantly better functionality, ease of use and fit with customers' needs. Good is not good enough.

- **Value proposition is lacking** – Most of the companies we meet lack a value proposition; or their proposition is too generic, weak, or unpersuasive. The most compelling value proposition articulates a clear economic value for a specific customer profile. Sophisticated customers are not looking for generic solutions, nor are investors.

- **Customer acquisition is not repeatable or scalable** – In markets with lots of potential customers, startups need to focus on a clear initial customer set. We meet lots of entrepreneurs who don't understand the importance of product/market fit, nor the process for finding that ideal fit. All too often, they believe they can sell to anyone and everyone—an approach that is unrealistic in large markets such as the U.S. Additionally, some sort of market validation is almost always necessary to demonstrate that the company knows how to sell, and to whom. Even later-stage companies we've worked with have found that the U.S. market is almost always different from their home markets when it comes to whom you sell, *how* you sell, and *which* channels of distribution you use. You need all these elements in place to create a repeatable, scalable process for identifying prospects and closing sales.

- **Incomplete team** – The management teams of many startups lack one or more key people with the requisite skills and domain expertise to operate in U.S. markets. Some of this expertise can be acquired by hiring U.S. employees or by bringing on advisors or board members. However, the CEO needs to take a hands-on role in identifying product-market fit, selling to customers and meeting with investors to raise capital. The model of the CEO as a "general manager" who hires someone to handle sales or raise capital does not and will not work in Silicon Valley.

Recommendations for All Silicon Valley Visitors

Visiting Silicon Valley requires significant advance planning and preparation. Be thoughtful about why you're visiting, what you hope to accomplish, and whom you want to meet. It's also important to plan the follow-up after your visit.

We wrote this chapter specifically to share some insider tips about what you should do, what you should watch out for, and how you can set realistic goals and expectations. Our intention is to help you maximize your learning experience in Silicon Valley. Regardless of your reasons for visiting the Valley, here are some essential things you need to do before your trip.

- **Before your visit:**
  - Talk to others in your region who have recently visited Silicon Valley. They will have the most up-to-date information and may be able to provide contacts, introductions and suggestions for your visit.
  - Update your LinkedIn personal and company profiles. If they are not already in English, translate them—carefully.
  - Ensure that your website and sales tools are up to date; and if they're not in English, translate these, as well.

- Determine if there are conferences and events that would make sense to attend, and schedule your trip around them.

- Ensure that you have business cards in English. A U.S. phone number helps.

- **During your visit:**

  - Listen carefully for the Silicon Valley perspective on how companies are built. The questions we ask and the concerns we raise about what you're doing may be different from what you've heard elsewhere.

  - Be aware that what you've read about Silicon Valley as recently as six months ago may be out of date and no longer representative of what's happening now.

  - Seek out a broad range of people to meet and talk with. People in Silicon Valley tend to have eclectic backgrounds, diverse work experiences, and non-obvious colleagues in their networks. And no one here knows everything.

  - Ask lots of open-ended questions as a way of gaining deeper insight into the concerns, perspectives and frame of reference of the persons to whom you're talking.

  - Be open to feedback, recognizing you'll get conflicting advice and differing points of view.

  - Be on time for your scheduled meetings. Do a time check before the meeting starts, and start and finish on time. Meetings must have a clear purpose. It's important not to waste people's time.

  - If you receive guidance or introductions, ask how you can reciprocate. Then do so.

  - Recognize that there is no clear roadmap to what you're trying to achieve here. It takes time and a bit of luck.

  - Realize how your own culture, values, biases and attitudes influence your thinking and your approach to building a business.

  - After each interaction, write down and *follow through* on next steps. It's too easy to forget what you intended or committed to do.

– Be thoughtful about how you spend your time, and prioritize your activities to support your objectives and goals.

- **After your visit:**

    Many entrepreneurs from outside the Valley are guilty of not staying in touch with the contacts they worked so hard to make during their visit here. One prominent VC we know, who is originally from Europe, is frequently sought out by government officials and entrepreneurs from his home country when they visit Silicon Valley. His comment to us: "They come here, they meet with me and I never hear from them again. After I host them, I'm treated like a fire hydrant." Yep, you're visualizing that correctly. As important as it is to prepare for your visit, what you do *afterward* is in some ways even more important. If you plan to sell to customers, develop partnerships, or raise capital in the Valley, you need to follow up, follow through and stay in touch.

    It takes work to maintain your network. A simple thank-you email is appropriate (and appreciated) after your meeting. If a person offered to make an introduction for you that you're *not* ready for, you need to say so: "Thank you for your kind offer to introduce me to [name]. However, I won't be ready for that intro until we do [XX]. I hope your offer will still be available in [YY] months."

    Extend an invitation on LinkedIn to the people you've met. Engage with them on social media and follow them on Twitter and Facebook, as appropriate. It's okay to let people know what's going on with your company when something relevant happens, but this does *not* mean sending a detailed email every week or month, unless it's to someone who has specifically asked for that amount of information or level of frequency. Sending an update quarterly, or maybe twice a quarter if there's a lot of progress, is more than sufficient. If you do provide an update, it should contain information that's relevant to the recipient; otherwise it will be ignored and deleted.

Once you're back home, debrief your team on what you've learned, and set out a series of next steps. Regardless of the reason for your visit, you've likely acquired a new perspective on your business. Remember all those notes we suggested you make? Go over them, asking yourself:

- What did I learn in Silicon Valley, and how can I apply it to our company?
- How has my thinking changed regarding how to build and scale the company?
- What should I start doing differently?
- How should our goals and priorities change?

"It's not such a dangerous place." – Lene Sjorslev Schulze

Lene Sjorslev

Lene Sjorslev Schulze is business catalyst at 42 Associates, cofounder of Nordic Innovation House and former deputy director of Innovation Center Denmark.

Working with more than 100 Danish companies as part of the ScaleIT program at Innovation Center Denmark, Lene noticed that many entrepreneurs have serious misconceptions about fundraising in Silicon Valley. "Entrepreneurs know there's lots of money here, and they think it's easily accessible," she remarks. "They don't take into consideration all the work that goes into raising capital.

"I would regularly receive emails from Danish entrepreneurs who'd say, 'We're coming to Silicon Valley in two weeks. Will you help us get meetings with these ten investors on Sand Hill Road?' But those entrepreneurs typically hadn't done the necessary research. They'd list a bunch of investors, many of whom didn't invest in the appropriate sector.

"I would tell them that a better way to start would be to figure out how Silicon Valley works, to do the necessary preparation of their business to be funded (which is a long road), and to commit themselves to being here to build their business. If you talk to the most successful Danish entrepreneurs, that's how they've made it.

"Some Danish entrepreneurs seeking capital go back and forth regularly [between Copenhagen and Silicon Valley] looking for seed or first-round financing, which is very expensive. They should find that financing *first* in Denmark, and build a healthy business in their home region before coming to the Valley.

"The way we do business here is unfamiliar to many entrepreneurs outside of the Valley. The whole networking thing, the open-mindedness, the pay-it-forward attitude, and the support for entrepreneurs—all seem odd to outsiders. People are intimidated. But by coming here, spending a week, and figuring out how it all works, and then by sitting down with some successful Danish entrepreneurs such as Mikkel Svane, CEO of Zendesk, and hearing how these entrepreneurs got started, helps. Just a few years before, these entrepreneurs were sitting in someone's kitchen in Copenhagen building a product. They come here and hear success stories, and the experience eliminates their fears. They see that Silicon Valley is not such a dangerous place."

Improving Your Effectiveness

Entrepreneurs come to Silicon Valley for a variety of reasons, including these:

- To see and learn
- To raise capital
- To conduct market validation and sales
- To evaluate or join an accelerator program
- To begin a company relocation process

Each of these reasons makes good sense. However, each necessitates a different level of commitment by the company management team in terms of time and money. For example, seeing and learning usually takes a time commitment of one to two weeks and costs a few thousand dollars, while relocating your business in order to scale a U.S. sales effort can take a couple of years and require upward of a million dollars.

We understand that everyone has different objectives for visiting Silicon Valley. Here are some specific suggestions for your consideration before, during and after your visit to Silicon Valley, based on individual objectives.

- **Seeing and Learning** – Most visitors to the Valley come to look around, attend events, meet people and learn. However, given the limited amount of time most people have, these visits rarely allow the visitor to internalize all the subtleties of Silicon Valley. In some ways, these visits are more like trips to Disney World—interesting and exciting, but difficult to derive significant long-term business value from. During an initial trip, you may develop more realistic objectives about what you can do in the Valley, along with a better sense of whom you need to meet on a follow-up trip.

  If you're based outside the U.S., your government may have trade offices or other resources that can assist you during your visit. We have worked with many of these organizations, including Apex Brasil, Innovation Center Denmark, Invest Northern Ireland, and Kotra/KIC of Korea, to name a few. Each has its own capabilities and unique network of contacts, which can be a great starting point if you're looking for a cofounder, certain service professionals, or strategic advisors. These organizations understand the cultural differences you may face and often can connect you to others from your region now located in the Valley.

  If you're a U.S.-based company visiting the Valley, there are not a lot of resources or government entities that can help you. Your best bet is to reach out to fellow entrepreneurs who have visited the Valley in the past six months for advice, guidance and contacts.

- **Raising Capital** – A significant number of entrepreneurs we meet have come to Silicon Valley specifically to raise capital. Most are not ready. Among those who are, many do not understand that the first step in raising capital is *learning how* to raise capital in Silicon Valley. Investors have their own specific criteria for investment. They often differ on the types of company they invest in, the stage of growth at which they invest and the amount of capital they are willing to invest. Most investors want their potential investees to have formed U.S. corporations and to have put in place U.S. management prior to being pitched. If your management team isn't in Silicon Valley and you do not yet have U.S. customers, the number of potential investors who'll seriously consider an investment drops dramatically.

We recently met with a startup team from Denmark who came to Silicon Valley specifically to raise capital. They had a 26-slide presentation, yet had no idea what their U.S. market entry strategy would be, nor who would be part of the U.S. team to implement the strategy. Their assumption was that they could answer these questions and issues after they raised capital. This company was not ready to talk with investors. Their visit would have been much more productive if they had thought through their U.S. market entry plans before meeting with investors.

> *Every Silicon Valley investor has a unique set of investments—with preferences for different sectors. You have to ask: How does my startup fit in this investor's network?*
>
> – Balazs Farago, Real5D

The number-one issue we hear from venture investors who meet with entrepreneurs from outside the region is that they have not done their homework. You need to understand who your competitors are, which markets they address, how they are positioned and which venture firms have invested in them.

"Do your homework." – John Scull

John Scull

John Scull is a venture capitalist at Southern Cross Ventures.

Years ago when John Scull started his first company—a predecessor to Macromedia—he moved from Chicago to San Francisco to be closer to the creative and tech communities in Silicon Valley. His first venture capital investor was John Doerr at Kleiner Perkins. By securing an investment from Doerr, he gained instant credibility in the Valley, which made it easier for him to recruit people and find early customers. This wouldn't have happened had he secured funding from a Chicago investor.

"You need to be able to see (and be seen in) Silicon Valley, and to build contacts," Scull advises entrepreneurs coming to the Valley. "Silicon Valley operates best when entrepreneurs use it as a network to get introductions and foster relationships. If I'm contacted directly, I'll often have coffee with an entrepreneur. But the entrepreneur only gets one shot. Entrepreneurs need to do their homework and tell me: What does the business look like? What is the market opportunity? Who are your competitors? Why is the U.S. a good market for you? Do your homework.

"You've also got to find the right person at the right firm to talk to. The problem is that most entrepreneurs outside the region don't know who's interested in their specific business. That's why they need mentors—to help them find a good fit. When a VC meets an entrepreneur and likes him, he'll try to introduce the entrepreneur to the right people. But VCs won't make introductions if there's no fit. Those over thirty-five years of age tend to be protective of their networks, while people under thirty-five are willing to make introductions freely—but they often do so without endorsing the people they are introducing.

"And there's one more reason why it's important to be here: If you're not in the area, it's hard for others to do reference checks on you. Sometimes we'll do reference checks through the local ex-pat community if the company is from abroad."

About raising capital, Scull says: "When you're looking to raise financing of $1 to $3 million, you should anchor it with smart money. It doesn't all have to be smart money, but you want some because you want people supporting you who can introduce you to contacts and connections in your market, and provide you with help and mentoring. For a round of financing between $500,000 and $3 million, there's lots of money available through angels and micro-VCs running $25 to $50 million funds. You can find angel investors by networking through incubators such as Y Combinator and 500 Startups; or by contacting angel groups such as Sand Hill Angels, Silicon Valley Angels, and Harvard Angels. The $75 to $250 million funds really want to put their money into Series A financing."

> *Never say that you don't have competition. You're not that interesting if you don't have competition...*
>
> – Lene Sjorslev Schulze, 42 Associates

Silicon Valley isn't the place to utter the words "we have no competition." No one here believes that, and if you say it, your credibility will be questioned. Competition comes in many forms: direct or head-to-head challenges from another product or company; indirect competition from broader product or service offerings; and competition in the form of inaction or paralysis on the part of customers—often the consummate deal-killer. Competition always exists in one form or another.

VCs in Silicon Valley are interested in meeting with founders of innovative startups. However, these companies need to fit with the VCs' sector of interest and geographic constraints in order to be of genuine interest, and they need to be ready for venture investment. If you're planning to meet with a venture capitalist, you need to review that person's LinkedIn profile, review the portfolio listing on his or her company's website and do some research on TechCrunch or LinkSV.

> *" The secret to raising money? Gain some business traction first since that trumps everything. Raise money when you don't need it. "*

> – Chris Yeh, PBWorks

Here are some suggestions to make the fundraising process easier:

- Talk to fellow entrepreneurs who have already raised capital.

- Create a succinct executive summary and a 10-slide deck.

- Identify other companies in your sector, especially those that are venture-backed.

- Realistically assess which investors will be interested in your company, recognizing that a majority of Silicon Valley investors will only invest in Silicon Valley/U.S. companies and management teams.

- Identify the pitch events and activities you want to attend as an observer to learn what works and what doesn't.

Unless you've successfully raised capital in Silicon Valley, our recommendation is that you come here with the primary objective of *learning how to raise capital*, rather than initially trying to raise it. This means that in your first visit you're unlikely to raise capital—unless you meet someone in one of those random, happy accidents. Your time here should be spent attending pitch events (to see both good and bad presentations) and developing a better understanding of how the fundraising process works. Attending conferences and events can also provide insight into your competitive landscape.

Here are some additional things to remember:

- If you are pitching to investors, we encourage you to look at Chapter 3 and refer to the Appendix A and B for other resources that can help make you more effective in what you present and how you present it.

- If you have the opportunity to present, listen carefully to the questions and concerns directed toward your company. Which ones are important? Should you make changes to your business model, your target market or the composition of your management team as a result of what you hear?

- Begin identifying the resources and personnel in Silicon Valley who can help you—including mentors, advisors, lawyers or other service professionals.

- Decide if you're ready to go through the full fundraising process. It's time consuming, and it generally requires relocation of the business beforehand and adequate capital to support your endeavor. If you decide that Silicon Valley investors currently are not right for your company, consider the following:

  - Are there other funding options that may make more sense, such as initially raising capital in your own region? Doing so might allow you time and resources to build a U.S. customer base and management team before you raise a round of capital in the U.S.

  - Does joining an incubator or accelerator in Silicon Valley or elsewhere make better sense for you and your company? Doing so can enable you to sort out the product/market fit, generate some initial customer traction and secure introductions to potential investors through the accelerator's network.

  - Will spending more time in Silicon Valley enhance your understanding of the market, your target customers and your potential investors? We've met many founders who choose this course so they can broaden and deepen their network and understand the subtleties of Silicon Valley.

The best money is the customer's money. If a startup has customers and sales, it doesn't need investors.

– Balazs Farago, Real5D

Validating the Market and Closing Sales

Just as the first step in raising capital is to understand *how to raise capital*, we believe the first step to selling into large, complex markets such as Silicon Valley or the U.S. is to *validate the market*. Market opportunities in the entire U.S. are rarely the same as market opportunities in your own region. If you already know how to validate the market, great. If not, go back to Chapter 5 where we cover product/market fit.

We have some additional suggestions on how to do market validation and make sales in the U.S. market. While some of this may be obvious or repetitive, this issue is the single biggest stumbling block that companies deal with.

In our experience, companies most successful in entering the U.S. market are those that have already gained customer traction and revenues in their home regions. Doing so forces a discipline within the organization that requires the team to build a product that works, define a repeatable sales process and clearly quantify the customer value proposition.

The process of validating the U.S. market is one of discovery: You formulate a hypothesis, and then you validate, change, and refine it based on your meetings, discussions, and networking. While online research is recommended, the only way to get definitive answers is by talking to those in your target market. Below are a number of ways to expedite the process of identifying and validating your market here.

- If you're located outside the U.S., contact your local government trade office to understand what resources may be available to you.

- Conduct in-depth primary research on the U.S. market size, customers' requirements and potential competitors.

- Determine who you think your first U.S. customers will be. Research them. Where are they located? Make necessary refinements to your target customer profile based on what you learn. Your sales materials and presentations should be tailored to your target customers here.

- Schedule prospective customer and partner meetings well in advance of your visit—weeks, not days in advance!

- Develop a list of relevant people you want to connect with. Most of us are only a few clicks away on LinkedIn. Be realistic about who is on your list. Famous personalities and CEOs are generally inaccessible—and are not necessarily the right people to meet with, in any case.

- Identify seminars, conferences, and vertically focused events you might attend in the Valley, events where you can learn and network.

Market validation does *not* mean selling. If your goal is to understand the U.S. market and who your customer should be, then listening and learning should be your objective. If you go into a meeting with the intention of asking for a contract or closing a sale, you will get an answer—*yes* or *no*—but you will fail to get the helpful information you need. If you go under the guise of seeking information or guidance and then proceed to hard-sell the customer, your meeting can backfire; and if that happens you may seriously jeopardize your relationship with the person who made the introduction, as well as your ability to secure follow-on introductions from your network.

Sand Hill road in Menlo Park, home to many venture capitalists

"What makes success in a small market can kill you in a big one." – Viki Forrest

Viki Forrest

Viki Forrest is CEO of ANZA, an organization that helps Australian startups interested in entering the U.S. market and raising capital.

"Entrepreneurs in other regions often overvalue the success they've achieved in their home regions—and frequently, they believe they can come to Silicon Valley and replicate it here. But what makes them successful in a small market can kill them in a big one. For example, in small markets there's often plenty of time to do deals; but in Silicon Valley, the pace of transactions is anything but slow. Second, in small markets many entrepreneurs rely on a direct sales model since often they know all their customers; but the company will never scale in the U.S. if they rely on selling directly. They must consider channels.

"There is also a lack of understanding among outsiders of the collaborative nature of large markets. In the Valley, you can be competitive in one deal, and then partner with the same competitor in another. This is in contrast to small markets where everyone holds things close to the vest, and entrepreneurs are only looking to win business for themselves.

"In small markets, growing a business generally requires making small, incremental steps. But in Silicon Valley, growing a business requires bold, high-risk steps. A big, scalable business requires capital and a completely different way of managing. The best solution for outsiders, then, is to put the right people in place. Successful founders from outside the Valley often hire cofounders in Silicon Valley, people who are familiar with the nature of large markets.

"What is the biggest mistake entrepreneurs make? Raising capital here before building the business. You need to build and prove your business first—and that takes six months to a year."

Big companies in Silicon Valley, and increasingly across the U.S., are interested in innovation. They often have a greater willingness to work with startups, and they are often early adopters of technology. However, these companies have limited bandwidth for meetings that may not be core to their business. While you may want to get a guided tour of Facebook, Google, or LinkedIn, it is important to realize that the people at these companies need to spend time building their own businesses, and not necessarily helping you build yours. You need to ask: "Is my idea, product, or business far enough along to fit with the size and complexity typical of these large corporations? What's in it for them? Will my idea move the needle—that is, have a big impact on their business?" If the answer is not the affirmative to all three questions, then securing those meetings will be much more difficult. We have been asked by entrepreneurs to arrange meetings with Google engineering to "talk deeply about their products." Rarely is this kind of meeting an important priority for a company such as Google.

If you do succeed in attracting the attention of a large company here, remember this: most of the initial decision-making in these large, complex corporations happens at the divisional or product level, even though final decisions often remain at the corporate level. For that reason, networking through engineering or product management is almost always more effective than meeting with the CEO.

Here are some further suggestions about those meetings:

- Ask specific questions, but make them all open-ended. Inquire about how the company currently solves the problem, what the cost of that problem is, whether the company might value the solution delivered by a product such as yours, whether they believe you have the right pricing structure, and how they evaluate and make decisions about new products (who manages the budget, and so forth).

- Unless the person you talk to expresses interest as a customer, request referrals and introductions to other people. Ask how you can reciprocate.

After your initial set of meetings, your job is to figure out what makes sense—including rethinking your product or target customer profile. Decide if you need to talk to customers with a different profile. The goal of market validation is to understand who you'll pursue as customers, where they are located, and how you will reach them. You also need to think about what you can afford to do.

So what's next? Here are some final questions to ask yourself in the market validation part of the process:

- Is the U.S. market the right market for me?
- How much time and money will it take to enter the U.S. market?
- Do I need to raise capital, and where is the best place to do this?
- Who are the right initial customers?
- Which are the right markets, geographies, and channels of distribution?

Based on the answers to these questions, revise and refine your target customer profile.

Rosewood Hotel in Menlo Park

If you're serious about building a market in Silicon Valley or the entire U.S., you have to build a strategy that doesn't assume you will periodically parachute into Silicon Valley. You need full-time, committed resources to be successful.

> *The biggest mistake entrepreneurs make is to horribly misjudge the time it takes to get things done here. They say, 'I have to make this happen in three months,' but most people in the Valley won't invest in a relationship unless they know you're going to stick around for a while. Too many entrepreneurs try to force or rush things; they don't allow things to happen organically. It's like walking into a bar with the intention of finding a wife that night.*

– Derek Anderson, Startup Grind

Assessing Accelerator Programs

While the past decade has seen the rapid growth of incubation and acceleration programs both in Silicon Valley and around the world, the concept of accelerator programs has been around for at least twenty years. One early example was Idealab, which was founded in 1996 with Internet 1.0 successes and failures. Today, incubation and acceleration programs are supported by nonprofit enterprises such as Endeavor; corporations such as Johnson & Johnson, Tata, and Telefonica; and privately owned, stand-alone organizations such as Y Combinator and TechStars. Other programs include those run by coworking spaces such as GSVlabs and Runaway Accelerator, or by accelerators tied to venture capital funds such as 500 Startups. Each program offers different capabilities and different kinds of help. Sector-specific programs include those for hardware at Highway1;

for wearable technology at Wearable World; and for financial technology at Finextra, supported by Silicon Valley Bank/MasterCard. All vary in reputation, program length, amount of equity exchanged for cash, and help offered to startups.

> *One thing that has been successful for GSVlabs has been to align by verticals. This allows us to develop deep expertise in each vertical. Ed tech and sustainability are our two strongest verticals.... Our 'secret sauce' may be building these curated, connected communities.*
>
> – Diane Flynn, GSVlabs

We would like to share a perspective on accelerators. We see a growing mindset among entrepreneurs that an accelerator is the sole path to success for startups, particularly those that are located outside of Silicon Valley. We believe that entrepreneurs are not spending enough time identifying their own level of readiness, and they are not evaluating accelerator programs based on the programs' fit with their company. Too many entrepreneurs are simply looking at high-profile successes such as AirBnB and Uber coming from Y Combinator and using that data as their sole criterion for picking a program.

Here's a list of factors that we believe entrepreneurs should consider as they evaluate accelerators:

- **Fit** – We understand the appeal of certain brand-name accelerators. But you have to dig down into the services offered by an accelerator to ensure a good fit with what you actually want and need.

  What stage is your company? The kind of help your startup needs will be very different in the idea stage or product-introduction phase vs. a company that already has developed product, customers, and significant revenues in its home region.

Where is the accelerator located? If you're in certain industries, location matters. Startups with social and mobile apps might do well in Silicon Valley, while startups with insurance and investment banking solutions might be better suited to Boston or New York City.

Have you defined your goals? What do you hope to achieve while in the program? What help do you really need? What issues with your product, product/market fit, go-to-market strategy, team members, or investment needs do you need help with? What are the shortcomings of your team, your product, your company? How much time do you have? What alternatives are available to you in terms of time and cost?

Programs vary widely, ranging from weeks to months. Finding that ideal match increases your chances of a successful outcome. And talking to others who have been through a program will help you better understand the differences between one program and another—which will ultimately help you decide what is best for your company.

- **Education** – Many accelerators and incubators offer some sort of entrepreneurial education or training activities as part of their programs. These range from formal, academic teaching to anecdotal talks and "war stories" from founders, investors, and others. "Ad hoc" talks on specific topics such as digital marketing and social media are also common. (Here's the challenge with the "war story" programs: Entrepreneurs have a great deal of difficulty figuring out how to apply such information to the specifics of their own businesses and the issues they are trying to address.)

We think the best programs are hybrids of these two approaches— programs that offer theory, plus practical and tactical best practices that entrepreneurs can use in building their businesses. Such programs, which typically run from a few days to a week, include candid assessments of a startup's business while highlighting gaps and challenges. They provide tools for the entrepreneur, and they identify specific areas where follow-on mentoring will add the greatest value. By bringing together many startups in an intensive, shared learning setting, they also create a unique opportunity for peer learning among founders.

- **Tough Love** – Founders need lots of support and encouragement, something that accelerators do well. However, in our experience, founders also need *tough* love. They need to be reminded when they have lost their focus; they need to be held accountable; and sometimes they need to be prodded into action, to move faster, to get stuff done. All this needs to be done in a way that motivates, rather than discourages them. And sometimes it is challenging for accelerator staff to provide that kind of tough love, since they have to work with founders every day. You benefit most from impartial advisors who can provide perspective and practical candor.

- **Mentors** – The best mentors understand their role, know how to be effective in working with a startup, and know where they can add the greatest value. In a similar way, startups need to understand the capabilities and limitation of mentors. A good mentor asks questions that raise issues in a constructive manner. He or she is a trusted sounding board for the founder—someone who provides tough love. A good mentor does *not* tell the CEO what to do and is not someone you call once a year. The best mentors bring deep experience in the startup world and may also bring specific domain expertise.

  Someone once observed that there are three categories of mentors: *grandfather, father,* and *mother*. A *grandfather* tells you "war stories," a *father* tells you what to do, and a *mother* asks you thoughtful, probing questions. Regardless of which accelerator program you join, make sure you find mentors who are good *mothers* and can help identify what you've missed.

  As a team that has trained mentors around the world (many of whom lack direct startup experience), we know that mentors who understand the startup process and its associated challenges are *better* mentors. In Silicon Valley, most mentors have prior startup experience. In other regions, many mentors do not, but if they receive proper training and have the right mindset, they can be very valuable to startups.

  The best incubators and accelerators have been thoughtful about bringing in people who can provide valuable expertise to startups and get those companies to the next stage in their business. However, we regularly see accelerator websites that list as mentors senior corporate executives and entrepreneurs-in-residence (EIRs) who we know simply don't have the time or bandwidth to work with startups. Most are working on their own companies, and if they're not, they are often looking to join a startup, not necessarily spending time helping another startup.

We appreciate that incubators and accelerators can be the right option for startups. Many high-profile successes, including Dropbox and AirBnB, have come out of formal accelerator programs. But there are also countless companies that have gone through these programs and then stalled or failed. And many companies that were never part of a formal accelerator program—Skype, Pinterest, and Facebook, for example—have succeeded wildly.

- **Relocation** – There is an undeniable mystique to Silicon Valley as a destination for entrepreneurs and startups. As we've observed, Silicon Valley works best for companies with global market potential. In our experience, companies with initial market traction in their home regions will more easily and quickly figure out how to be successful in the U.S. market. Entrepreneurs with only a product concept will find progress in the Valley much more difficult.

Does relocation really makes sense for you now? If not, when? Here are some things to do if you're thinking about relocating to Silicon Valley:

  – Consider this fact: Raising capital in your home region may be easier and faster than in Silicon Valley particularly if you have customers there.

  – Make sure you've done enough market validation prior to making a relocation commitment.

  – Get introductions from fellow entrepreneurs and trusted advisors to professional help in the Valley—especially to corporate, tax, and immigration lawyers.

- Determine which part of your organization should *not* relocate to the U.S.

- Consider shared office space as a way of assimilating into Silicon Valley and interacting with local entrepreneurs.

- Build a Silicon Valley board of advisors.

- Understand that selling your product will initially be the responsibility of the CEO of your company. The CEO needs to validate the sales process and the target customer. It is only later that you can supplement your sales process with local personnel.

- In an enormous market such as the U.S., plan to leverage your sales efforts through distribution channels, partners, and strategic alliances.

- Align your compensation plan, including salaries and stock allocation, with Silicon Valley norms.

Caveats

Being effective in Silicon Valley requires that you use your time efficiently. Here are five things to keep in mind as you do business in the Valley.

- **Think before you pay for introductions.**

  You will find lots of people here interested in helping you, and there are certain categories of help you should expect to pay for. Lawyers, accountants, recruiters, and professionals helping you to raise capital or to build a better presentation should all be paid for their work. But you should not be paying for introductions that are made on your behalf.

  For example, if someone makes a quick introduction to a lawyer or a venture capitalist (an email that you have already written, giving reasons for the introduction), you should not have to pay. If anyone wants to charge you for sending a couple of emails, think through the situation carefully; in most cases, it doesn't make sense.

- **Beware of faux investors.**

  A small but visible minority of venture capitalists and angels have made no investments in the past twenty-four-plus months. They often have no funds to invest. We call these people faux VCs and faux angels. Some make their living as recruiters; others give war-story speeches at every venue that will pay them to perform; and some don't have a job and are looking for their next gig. They often lead entrepreneurs on under the guise that they will invest.

  It's important to be direct. If you suspect you are talking to a faux investor, ask about their recent investments, track record, and successes before you spend time pitching your company. If their recent investment activity took place more than a year ago, chances are high that they are actually trading on a legacy from prior years. Your time is a nonrenewable resource. Use it wisely.

- **Remember quid pro quo.**

  Silicon Valley is known for its *pay-it-forward* mentality, one in which people who have achieved success offer to help other entrepreneurs. It's true. It happens. We practice it.

  Still, visitors to Silicon Valley too often fail to understand it is *not all free* here. The Silicon Valley community expects that an offer of help will be reciprocated. An email introduction on your behalf merits—at minimum—a "thank you." It also requires that you follow through on that introduction, arrive promptly for that meeting, and circle back to the person who made the introduction with feedback on the meeting and any next steps.

  Many service professionals help startups with marketing, accounting, and legal services; and almost all these providers expect entrepreneurs to pay them for their time and expertise. If a lawyer does a favor for you by providing you with a standard confidentiality agreement gratis, you need to reciprocate with at least a "thank you." Further, when you need to hire a lawyer in the future to undertake significant work, such as incorporation or a written contract, the lawyer who did you a favor should—at the very least—have the first shot on bidding for that business. Referring another startup to the lawyer can be a form of quid pro quo.

We have heard stories of VCs who meet a very engaging entrepreneur with a compelling business opportunity. The VC spends time with the entrepreneur, making introductions and connecting that person to angel investors. Yes, this help may be "free." But most investors in this situation expect to be offered access to the deal when the company is ready to raise venture capital. Visitors who expect service, expertise, and guidance for free are increasingly becoming sore points among Valley insiders.

And most visitors don't fully understand the fundamental difference between *pay it forward* and *quid pro quo*. Pay it forward means offering small, helpful favors that don't require a lot of time or resources as a payback for the same kinds of favors others have offered to you. Quid pro quo means appropriately rewarding people when they provide you with real work requiring meaningful amounts of their time. Always recognize, acknowledge, and appropriately reward people who help you.

Yelp offices in San Francisco

- **Be careful of pitching fees.**

  There are a small number of not-for-profit and for-profit groups that charge entrepreneurs for the privilege of pitching to investors. As an entrepreneur seeking financing, should you pay for these services? It depends. Ask yourself: Does the group provide references of startups that have found investment through these pitches? Are the investors to whom you'd be introduced likely to have an interest in your product or market sector? How much money might they invest? Will these investors lead a round of financing, or are they the kind who wait for a lead investor before agreeing to put money into a company? If you pay to pitch, you should be connected to the right audience, and the agreement must offer you the right cost/benefit ratio. Remember: There are lots of opportunities to pitch both formally and informally at no charge.

  Some individuals will offer to raise capital for you for a fee. Once again, ask yourself: Will they do real work for you, or will they simply give you a list of potential investors and expect you to do all the work? Will they simply email your business plan to a (qualified or unqualified) list? Startups that have indiscriminately had their plans sent to too many investors quickly gain the reputation of being "shopped"—and these startups tend to be of little interest to investors. Activities like this can hurt you. Think this one through carefully.

- **Avoid parachuting into Silicon Valley.**

  Many international entrepreneurs believe they can do business in the U.S. without first establishing a U.S. legal entity or local management team. They think that developing the market, forming partnerships, finding customers, and creating distribution channels can be done quickly and easily here. This is usually not the case. Getting customer traction takes time, and having a full-time U.S. presence will make this much easier.

  While the U.S. shares the same language, same currency, and a similar legal framework across all fifty states, there are significant differences in the culture and style of doing business in various parts of the country. There are twenty-five to thirty major metropolitan markets, many of which are larger in business potential than the GDP of many countries. California is currently the seventh largest economy in the world. What's more, U.S. metro areas tend to have company and industry concentrations *unique to their geographic regions*. For example, technology manufacturing takes place primarily in the lower-cost regions of the country—the Southeast, the Midwest, and parts of the Northeast. Very little manufacturing of technology-based products actually occurs in Silicon Valley. Similarly, most business in the financial services sector is based either in Chicago and or in the greater New York metro area. You need to be based where your customers and partners are located. You can't say to a customer or investors, "I'll see you next time I'm in town," and expect to get the deal.

We worked with an entrepreneur from Mexico who had developed an enterprise software application for the financial services industry. His target clients were large banks, insurance companies, brokerage firms, and wealth managers, most of which were based in New York City. However, he was insistent about being located in Los Angeles. L.A. is a six-hour flight from N.Y.C., and basing his company in L.A. required that he spend a full day of travel to get to his clients. We soon realized that he envisioned himself in a tuxedo on the red carpet attending the Oscars, and he believed that he needed to be based in Los Angeles to fulfill that dream. Clearly, his personal goals were inconsistent with the realities of his business.

In some regions of the world, selling is based more on *whom you know* than on *what you're selling*. Entrepreneurs from these regions often believe that a warm introduction to a customer or investor will clinch a sale or assure venture funding. But in reality, a warm introduction will give you only the opportunity for an audience. With a prospective customer, the purchase decision is based on the fit of the product to the customer's need and a thorough evaluation of the product relative to other products. And with a potential investor, the financing is based on the fit with the fund's investment criteria, and whether the investor likes the entrepreneur and believes in the business.

Silicon Valley Is Ready—Are You?

Some entrepreneurs are Silicon Valley naturals. They understand what it takes, what they need to do, and how to be effective in building and leveraging their network here. Others find Silicon Valley mystifying and confusing, need help getting connected, and have trouble putting all the pieces together. If you look more like a "natural," then we would encourage you to move quickly, trust your instincts, and leverage the expertise and resources of Silicon Valley to your advantage. However, if you're in the "mystified" category, then identifying the people and resources who can help you becomes even more important.

> *Relocate to Silicon Valley only if you're thinking about building a truly high-growth company.*

– Lene Sjorslev Schulze, 42 Associates

Silicon Valley is a wonderful place. We encourage you to come and visit—and, if appropriate, to stay. But it's not Disney World. It is a place where people work and live. And it's important that you adjust your perception to what is here, not to what you have heard or read. On any given day, hundreds—perhaps thousands—of visitors are in Silicon Valley to accomplish goals similar or identical to yours.

There's no straight path to investors, customers, or business success. The process of trial and error is continual. It's not about the cool offices, the office slide, the nap pods, or the delicious daily lunches. The more time you spend here, the more you find that it's about smart people and hard work. Silicon Valley is a great place to find a cofounder, meet thought leaders on the leading edge of technology, connect with other smart entrepreneurs at a meetup, or run into a venture capitalist at a local coffee shop. While there's a definite mystique to Silicon Valley, there is no magic to building a successful business. The more time you spend here, the clearer you become about what you need to do, how you need to go about it, and how you can improve your chances of success.

If you remain based in your own region, we want you to be able to leverage the Valley's best practices in your area. And if you do come to the Valley, we want you to be as well prepared as possible to get customers, develop partnerships, and raise capital. Our goal is to see your company successful wherever you may be.

CHAPTER 9

Everywhere Matters

Silicon Valley's success in building global businesses is based on a unique combination of ideas, people, mindset, culture, best practices, and capital. This creates an environment that enables entrepreneurs here to start and successfully grow global businesses.

For companies outside the region, leveraging Silicon Valley almost always requires some level of business success in your local region *first*. Without local traction, you will find it difficult, perhaps impossible, to effectively leverage Silicon Valley for capital, personnel, or expertise. This is almost always the case even if the company does have global potential.

And if you never come to the Valley at all, you can still learn from some of the best practices here, apply them in your local market, and use them to successfully build a business in your region. You must figure out what you need, determine which rules can and should be broken, and understand how to adapt your business tactics to your local market. Our purpose in writing this book is not to make you an expert on Silicon Valley. Rather, it is to highlight best practices, tactics, and resources that you can selectively apply to building your business wherever you are located. One thing we love about entrepreneurs is that when local market opportunities emerge and innovative technologies become available, resourceful entrepreneurs build companies.

The remainder of this chapter expands on the things you can do to build success locally wherever you are, because *everywhere matters*.

Entrepreneurs Need Lots of Help

The first step in building local success is to stop making excuses about what's missing and what doesn't work in your region. It's hard. We know this. It's risky. We understand that. Consider this: Your chances of building a local success are higher than your chances of building a global winner.

As entrepreneurs ourselves, we understand the challenges and struggles that entrepreneurs face. While entrepreneurs are truly superheroes, they need help to achieve their potential. Specifically, they need supportive ecosystems and a community of other entrepreneurs.

We've seen a number of government and private startup programs that have been successful in this endeavor—as well as some that have not. Startup Chile was determined to bring more entrepreneurs to its country, celebrate them, and create a critical mass of talent. Since the program kicked off in 2010, it has attracted more than 800 companies from over 64 countries, and has built a community of entrepreneurs that seems to be thriving. There's more that needs to be done to build a vibrant, self-sustaining ecosystem but we think Startup Chile has made great progress.

Nomadic entrepreneurs

Nevertheless, there are downsides to this global effort. As countries set up incentives to attract entrepreneurs to their locales, we have noticed an increase in the number of "nomadic entrepreneurs"—a counterproductive trend, to be sure. These entrepreneurs use startup competitions, prize money, and country-specific financial incentives to relocate their companies to a particular region. When the money runs out, the team relocates to a different region that offers a new set of financial incentives. This occurs when a region lacks sufficient sources of *follow-on venture financing and an appropriate customer base* for a startup to build a sustainable business in that region. Ultimately it is good for neither the entrepreneur nor the region.

A Recipe (but No Formula) for Building an Entrepreneurial Ecosystem

We recognize that every region is unique in terms of culture, values, style of doing business, and overall attitude toward entrepreneurship. And the specifics of how to grow and enhance an entrepreneurial ecosystem vary by region. But our work in the U.S. and around the world has shown us that there are six key elements that can improve the quantity, quality, and success of startups everywhere:

1. Audacious pragmatism about what can grow and succeed in your region

2. Experienced entrepreneurs and qualified senior management

3. A supportive community, with qualified mentors and educational programs for entrepreneurs

4. A "can do" attitude that focuses on success, not failure

5. A culture that provides permission to experiment and iterate

6. A critical mass of customers, such as corporations and government entities

What may surprise you is that venture capital is *not* on our list. Venture capital certainly can help companies grow and scale faster, but it is not the biggest challenge most startups face—at least initially.

Today it's easier and less expensive to fund a software company than it was 20 years ago. A little money can go a long way. A founder today can make a lot of progress before he seeks a round of funding from traditional venture investors. Atlassian is a $5 billion company that grew without venture capital money. The $100 million invested by Accel Partners was used to buy out some early shareholders, not to build the company. However it is important to remember that companies do grow and succeed without venture capital financing.

"If you build local...your impact will be exponentially greater." – Derek Anderson, Startup Grind

Derek Anderson

"You should be the best person in the world to solve the problem you're solving. If you are, you might win. But you must be authentic wherever you are. Entrepreneurs in other regions of the world should not try to be SnapChat or YikYak, nor should they try to be Facebook since they are not Mark Zuckerberg and they are not located in Silicon Valley. You can't build Twitter in Nairobi; it needed to be built here, by the people who built it—by Evan Williams, the blogging and communications expert. If Evan were in Nairobi, could he have built it? Unlikely.

"I love entrepreneurs who build local and stay local. If you build a billion-dollar company here, then Silicon Valley has another billion-dollar company. But if you build a billion-dollar company in the Congo, you change everything. Your impact will be exponentially greater."

Let's take a closer look at these six key elements:

1. Audacious pragmatism about what can grow and succeed in your region

Building success takes pragmatism, but it also takes a willingness to set audacious goals. It is paramount that you understand the resources and skills necessary for entrepreneurs to grow, and the fit between what they need and what's available in your ecosystem. Here are the questions to ask:

- **Expertise:** Are people with the right business experience and technical expertise available locally? Do you have the appropriate curated network to build your team, close customer contracts, and move your business forward?

- **Technology:** Are the necessary technologies readily available?

- **Money:** Is the requisite capital available—and in the appropriate amounts?

- **Geography:** Is the startup in the right geographic location and time zone? Are you leveraging the region's natural advantages, including local industries and resources? Is the pool of employees adequate? Is the necessary infrastructure in place? For example, if a startup wants to establish a data center, does it have a constant, reliable source of electricity?

- **Customers:** Are there sufficient local customers who are willing to buy from an unproven startup?

Too often, we find entrepreneurs who are trying to build businesses that don't fit well with their ecosystem. Classic recipes for failure include the founder who locates his startup in a region with no local customers; or the founder whose startup requires significant venture capital long before sufficient market validation and traction have been established. In regions where little or no early-stage risk capital is available, we recommend that founders figure how to fund the development themselves, find customers who are willing to pay to have the product built, or pursue another business! And we like to see a business model that factors in the scarcity of outside capital. Pricing monthly but billing annually, in advance, is one way to get cash into the business sooner.

Another recipe for failure is the founder trying to launch a company that competes with what's hot in Silicon Valley, or what's hot globally, rather than focusing on regional problems and opportunities. According to Joe Kennedy, chairman emeritus of Pandora, "We are in a world where customers can easily identify and buy the best product. So if you're planning to service markets that are global in scope, you have to build the best product. If you cannot be the best in the world, do something else." What's hot in Silicon Valley may be much more useful in determining *what not to do* than what to do.

Certain businesses do really well in Silicon Valley. It may be difficult, if not impossible, for those same businesses to succeed in another region. Being thoughtful, realistic, and pragmatic about what you start improves your chances of eventually building a successful company.

Of course, there are exceptions to all we've said here. We know companies that have succeeded despite the regions in which they were started. For example, Prezi—the presentation software company that has attracted more than 60 million users—is located in both Budapest and San Francisco. Other examples include successful clones of Uber, eBay, AirBnB, and Amazon that have started up in various regions of the world.

Many regions want to either replicate Silicon Valley's ecosystem or create an environment where large, Silicon Valley-sized companies can grow and prosper. The continuing challenge is how to do this. We see an impedance mismatch between what these regions want to achieve and the regional limitations, risk profile, and time frame in which success can be achieved. It all has to fit together, be realistic, and make sense.

Having worked with economic development agencies whose job it is to grow the number of entrepreneurs and startups in their regions, we have noticed two fundamentally different approaches to building a vibrant entrepreneurial ecosystem. One approach focuses primarily on building big successful startups, while the other focuses on building a deep pool of experienced entrepreneurs with a long-term goal of creating successful startups.

The "big hits" approach is one that focuses on building large, global companies that will exit through IPOs or acquisitions. Such companies typically require large amounts of venture financing, appropriate "adult supervision" (experience, guidance, support, and mentorship), a time frame of approximately eight years to grow to maturity, and a great deal of luck—since the probability of building such a company is measured in *fractions of a percent*. Skype, Alibaba, and Tencent are good examples of the "big hits" strategy. However, we want to emphasize that the probability of achieving these large successes remains low, and losers show up long before winners.

The second approach focuses on growing "good rootstock." In this approach, the primary goal in the short term is to create experienced entrepreneurs, not successful companies. These entrepreneurs start lots of companies with minimal capital, and gain valuable experience from the startup process. Since the reality is that most of these companies will fail, the entrepreneurs have the opportunity to learn from their mistakes, and the good ones go on to do better next time. A few entrepreneurs will succeed in building large, possibly global businesses. The rest may find success in their second, third, or fourth startup attempt. The advantage of the "good rootstock" approach is that little or no capital is invested in any one company until there is a clear product/market fit and evidence of *real* market traction.

While these two approaches are different, they are not mutually exclusive. In an ideal situation, a region would encourage many startups, hoping that one or more will become big winners, given enough time.

2. Experienced entrepreneurs and qualified senior management

Entrepreneurs are at the heart of an ecosystem. In every region, there are those that will take risks and start companies, regardless of whether the requisite talent, capital, and resources are readily available. And there are others who won't even think about becoming an entrepreneur. For a subset of this latter group, education and awareness can improve the probability that they will consider entrepreneurship in their career path.

> ❝ *Considering a startup as part of one's career path is not a view shared universally in the U.S. or globally. However, this will likely change over time.* ❞
>
> – Ann Winblad, Hummer Winblad Venture Partners

Formal entrepreneurial education in high school and college, coupled with relevant internships, is an effective way to improve the acceptability of entrepreneurship as a career path in many regions of the world. Targeted training for university professors, and educational programs in entrepreneurial centers such as Silicon Valley, can help broaden one's perspective and inspire innovation. Just as working for a large, well-known company can be prestigious, starting up a company should be equally lauded.

In the U.S., a range of TV shows and movies actually glamorizes entrepreneurs and their startups. They include the HBO show Silicon Valley, the ABC show Shark Tank, movies including The Social Network and The Interns, and older documentaries such as the 1999 film Startup. com. There are also dozens of books, movies, and documentaries profiling Steve Jobs, the late cofounder of Apple, for example. Education initiatives that use print, online, and entertainment channels to increase societal acceptance of startups and entrepreneurship can be useful in any region. If an ecosystem were to provide successful entrepreneurs with one-tenth the accolades provided to professional athletes, they would dramatically increase the number of entrepreneurs in their region over time. This has happened in Silicon Valley.

> *I learned a lot about sales, process, quality, and customer-centric organizations while working at Xerox. They had a tremendous commitment to training and I learned a great deal about how to scale. Today, entrepreneurs with corporate experience have a higher chance of success.*

– Kayvan Baroumond, SV101 Ventures

Where will entrepreneurs in *your* region come from? People who work at medium and large companies are often ideal candidates to take on the role of entrepreneur, since they bring to the task domain expertise, process knowledge, and a wealth of customer contacts and relationships. And if these individuals don't step forward and start companies, attracting entrepreneurs from elsewhere may be an option. While anecdotal evidence suggests that these *nomadic entrepreneurs* may remain in a country only so long as program funding is available, we know this approach provides some value in the short term.

Entrance to both Eventbrite and Slack Technologies offices in San Francisco

> *"[Startups are] chaotic places to work, with things changing on a whim."* – Ann Winblad

Ann Winblad

Ann Winblad is a cofounder and managing general partner at Hummer Winblad Venture Partners, a pioneering venture capital firm founded in 1989.

"If you want to get a taste of what it's like to become an entrepreneur, consider getting a job at a company such as Google, Facebook, or Amazon. These ten- to fifteen-year-old companies are at the top of their game, are going a zillion miles an hour, and everyone is accountable for something. They are chaotic places to work, with things changing on a whim—just like in a startup. New hires get formal training, and they find out if they have what it takes to start their own businesses. You find out quickly whether you have the intellectual and physical stamina to build something from scratch. Companies outside of Silicon Valley—Alibaba and AkInternet, for example—would serve the same purpose for entrepreneurs in other parts of the world."

3. A supportive community, qualified mentors, and educational programs for entrepreneurs

A supportive community is important for all entrepreneurs because they can and do learn a tremendous amount from one another. A collaborative community—one where "everyone is in it together"— helps to foster camaraderie. Shared workspaces, cafés, informal meetups, and get-togethers are all effective ways to build a community.

Many of the startup-readiness programs we have worked with in other regions promote the value of mentors. However, there is a dearth of experienced mentors who understand how to effectively add value to startups. We have been proactive in pushing formal mentor training as a way of building a critical mass of mentors that will provide help and guidance to startups in their region.

Mentors can come from many different backgrounds: Some are experienced entrepreneurs themselves, while others work in medium or large companies. In Silicon Valley, and increasingly around the world, service professionals also serve as startup mentors. They bring tremendous experience to startups, and they can help improve the overall ecosystem. In return, they benefit from tracking emerging companies, which can create a pipeline of opportunities for their own organizations.

A more strategic way to develop entrepreneurs is through education offered via programs and talks at shared workspaces, corporations, and the offices of service professionals. Even the best entrepreneurs can benefit from training programs that challenge them through classes that cover critical topics such as value proposition, product/market fit, and techniques for targeting the right customers and partners. These topics are, and will remain, key challenges for startups.

In many places outside of Silicon Valley, there are entrepreneurs who do take a risk and start a company. However, if it fails, the societal norms pin the blame for the failure on the entrepreneur: He *himself* is a failure. People do not understand that most companies in Silicon Valley—and elsewhere—*do fail*; it's up to the entrepreneur to keep trying until he finds the formula that succeeds. Entrepreneurs and the larger community need to understand that many Silicon Valley entrepreneurs have had one or more failures before achieving success.

In 2013, we presented the opening keynote for Eric Schmidt, Executive Chairman of Alphabet, Inc. (née Google), at a conference at Seoul National University in Korea. At that event, Schmidt summed up this point in one sentence: "Failure is a badge of learning." It is a sentiment we share.

4. A "can do" attitude that focuses on success, not failure

When we are asked to help develop entrepreneurial activities in a region, all too often we hear: "We can't start/succeed/grow because…." People point to a lack of capital, talent, mentors, or supporting partners; and they often complain that local attitudes and beliefs inhibit success. These statements may be true, but most people miss the bigger point. Don't fixate on failure. While it may be quite challenging to figure out how to accomplish something with less money, time, and resources, these constraints often lead to insight, creativity, innovation, and opportunity.

> *"Silicon Valley is a place of great freefalls. We are blind to the risk of failure until we hit the ground."*
>
> – Chris Shipley

Chris Shipley

Chris Shipley is a journalist, technology analyst, and former executive producer of the DEMO conference. She has worked with startups all over the world.

Chris Shipley expressed surprise and disappointment after attending Innovation Europe, the recent startup conference in Poland. Conference attendees were talking about the same things they'd discussed ten years ago. They lamented the lack of risk capital, and they complained about a host of other things that made it difficult—if not impossible—for them to launch successful startups. Silicon Valley is still being put on a pedestal as the *only* place one can succeed. Chris doesn't believe that. She believes that it is difficult to create a successful startup anywhere in the world—including Silicon Valley.

"The only real difference here," she comments, "is that Valley people are willing to take risks. Silicon Valley is a place of great freefalls. We are blind to the risk of failure until we hit the ground. People outside Silicon Valley are just as smart and have just as good ideas—if not better ones. They also have a cost advantage over the Valley. It is neither the lack of risk capital nor the ecosystem that holds these entrepreneurs back. Rather, it is the sense of hopelessness, and an unwillingness to take action. They rationalize by saying there is no risk capital. They complain that there are no mentors—but that's just code for 'I don't know what I am doing, so I will do nothing.' People get wrapped around the axles of what is *not* possible, instead of what *is* possible. But if you have nothing, what are you risking by taking a chance? There *are* investors, there *are* mentors—it's just that finding them takes more work outside Silicon Valley.

"It is easy to use the environment as your excuse: The cards are stacked against you, so don't even bother trying. But the irony is that the constraints are what lead to innovation! If you have the best engineers, managers, marketers, and so forth, then you don't have to work as hard. But if your college buddy and you are barely surviving on ramen noodles, then you have to think far more creatively about what you do. When I see Silicon Valley startups that have an espresso or margarita machine in the corner, I think that's two strikes against you. Those companies are focusing on the wrong things—and on the wrong use of capital.

"Cultural change is the hardest kind of all. In so many places, culture is steeped in family and tradition. All the startup competitions, all the efforts to promote entrepreneurship, will have minimal effect unless you look at those issues!

"So how do you change culture? It's a role model issue. You need to bring learning, education, and experience to your region. Silicon Valley is a state of mind as much as it is a geographic place. The entrepreneur from elsewhere says, 'I can't do it.' The Valley entrepreneur lives to find a way to make it happen.

"And policymakers need to consider how to build around the core competencies of their region. In the case of Boston, these core competencies are centered around hospitals and research. The universities have gotten smart about how to move stuff out of the labs. Faculty from MIT and elsewhere have become founders or cofounders of companies."

Many companies have been launched during depressions or recessions, including Microsoft, Hewlett Packard, CNN, and the Wikipedia Foundation. Cloudera and Uber, both founded in 2008 and 2009 respectively , survived the challenges of the global financial crisis. And other stories abound in which entrepreneurs succeed despite the limitations of the ecosystem, the economy, or the market.

This "can do" attitude can be promoted by profiling successful local or international entrepreneurs. They can become "celebrity rock stars," inspiring others through their stories of perseverance and success. At the same time, failed entrepreneurs can be useful in highlighting the fact that there is life after a failed startup—and it might be another startup.

> *In Silicon Valley, we have a culture of giving the entrepreneur the benefit of the doubt, initially. And because we do this, entrepreneurs think bigger and bolder.*
>
> – Kayvan Baroumand, SV101 Ventures

Entrepreneurs outside Silicon Valley too often focus on the possibility of failure instead of the opportunity for success. As a result, they hedge their bets and only do things half way. We know entrepreneurs who have decided to run two, even three, startups simultaneously because they are afraid that at least one company will fail. Instead of increasing their chances for success, this approach dramatically increases the probably of failure. Similarly, we see investors who are so concerned a company may fail that they strangle it with too little capital, even after the company has validated its market opportunity. This is another instance where fear of failure drives decision making in the wrong direction.

5. A culture that provides permission to experiment and to iterate

In Silicon Valley, permission to experiment is an integral part of the startup process, and we believe this is key to creating success in any entrepreneurial ecosystem. Building companies is all about experimenting on product, market, and product/market fit, and building a repeatable sales model *until you get it right.* The iteration and experimentation process, and a timeframe necessary to do this work, need to be embedded in the business plan. Similarly, investors need to understand that product/market fit and a repeatable sales model are almost always discovered through experimentation and iteration. This should be factored into the analysis during the investment decision-making process.

While it's natural for entrepreneurs to abbreviate their path to success as they tell their success stories, it's important for them to be forthcoming about the details of what they tried before they found their formula for success. Highlighting these stories and experiences in the media can be an effective way to create more awareness and appreciation for the length and challenges of the startup journey.

Finally, investors need to acknowledge that luck is frequently much more important than picking the right company to fund. More than one Silicon Valley investor has been quoted as saying that he would rather be lucky than smart.

6. A critical mass of customers in corporations and government entities

For entrepreneurs facing the challenges of identifying market opportunities, finding customers, and closing deals, large corporations and government agencies need to be open to purchasing products from startups. This means that the requirements and timetables built into the procurement process must be startup-friendly. We have seen instances where a requirement for five years of historical financial data effectively eliminated startups from vendor consideration.

There are many ways to align startups with local market needs. Hackathons have become effective ways to develop tailored solutions to public- and private-sector problems. They also provide the additional benefit of getting early buy-in from corporate and government sponsors. Governments can also offer incentives for corporations or agencies to purchase from startups, and they can create tax credits and policies that benefit startups.

In addition to the six components we've mentioned, a few other things are important to the development of an entrepreneurial ecosystem.

- **Sophisticated investors** – Having trained early-stage investors, we know that informed, savvy investors are good for startups and for a regional ecosystem. They help increase the chances of creating that next big, successful company. Investors who come strictly from a finance or banking background often focus on financial KPIs (key performance indicators) and other metrics that are less relevant to tracking the progress of an early-stage company. Entrepreneurs need investors who are empathic to the challenges of building a successful startup and can add value. Investors with prior startup experience are better able to help entrepreneurs across a broad spectrum of challenges.

  Educated angel and seed investors are particularly important to a successful, vibrant, and well-functioning startup environment. Early-stage investors can become better prepared through a range of programs, including locally based executive education and programs in Silicon Valley. These programs offer valuable peer learning that improves investors' chances of success in working with startups.

- **Tough love** – Even the best entrepreneurs—the ones who are laser focused in their plans—need practical candor and brutal honesty to help them sort through their options, make decisions, and progress toward their goals. This is what we call tough love.

  Tough love does not mean beating up a CEO because he missed a revenue target by 5 or 10 percent. It also does not mean revisiting a bad decision made six or twelve months earlier. The right kind of tough love helps the CEO understand what he or she has learned from having made a bad decision, and what he or she will do differently. It is asking such questions as *Is the 10 percent revenue shortfall this month going to be a 50 percent shortfall several months from now? Are there broader underlying problems that need to be addressed?*

CEOs frequently have no one in their companies with whom they can discuss the challenges they face. A CEO's relationship with his or her board is complicated, especially when board members may participate in future rounds of financing. In such situations, a CEO may not be entirely candid about the problems and challenges the company faces. Moreover, CEOs are always juggling too many tasks and goals simultaneously. Managing while multitasking is very difficult, especially for less-experienced CEOs. And CEOs are constantly being asked to make decisions with incomplete information. In such situations, the natural tendency is to postpone or avoid making the hard decisions. In all these scenarios, having a trusted confidant is important—especially one who offers tough love.

Something we see all too often is too much money being given to companies by unsophisticated investors or grant program administrators without the requisite level of adult supervision— or tough love. When these elements are lacking, entrepreneurs don't clearly think through their options, don't always make the tough choices, and are not always held accountable. This hurts the entrepreneurs' chances for success. Entrepreneurs need honest feedback to understand where they are, which issues they need to address, and how all the pieces of the business fit together.

We have been brought into leading acceleration programs around the world to teach master classes, and to troubleshoot the challenges facing these entrepreneurs. As part of that process, we've done readiness assessments for many startups that help pinpoint specific issues, weaknesses, and opportunities for these companies. The assessment and benchmarking tool we use extensively in our master classes is the G/ Score, developed by Chris Shipley, the journalist, technology analyst, and former executive producer of the DEMO conference. After hearing over 25,000 startup pitches, she became adept at identifying a company's current status, as well as its shortcomings, opportunities, and areas for growth and improvement. The G/Score is an effective tool for initiating a dialog about the issues a CEO faces. It's an excellent tool for mentors and investors, too. We have included it in Appendix C.

Silicon Valley is a place you can come to learn, and to find customers, partners, and capital. You may learn that you discover it anew every time you visit—because it's always changing. But remember: It is not the *be all* and *end all*.

The next steps are up to you. Instead of focusing on constraints, view them as catalysts for creativity, innovation, and resourcefulness in building your business. Forget about the things that can—and will—go wrong. Rather than focusing on all the ways in which you can fail, focus on achieving success.

This is the end of the chapter and the end of the book. We hope that this book will be part of the continuation of your journey as an entrepreneur building a successful company.

Entrepreneurs are everywhere. And everywhere matters.

Wherever you are, you need help and support. If we can assist you, let us know.

Appendix A – Resources

Here is a curated list of online sources of information, events, and articles that may be of value to you. There are many others. If you have a suggestion for additional links that we should include in future editions of this book, please let us know.

Events

SVForum runs monthly meetings and events that bring together startups, investors, corporations and others.
www.svforum.org

TiE is a worldwide organization with an active chapter in Silicon Valley that runs programs and sponsors an annual conference.
http://sv.tie.org/cevents

Silicon Vikings has programs that feature speakers on topics of interest to startups.
www.siliconvikings.com

Meetup lists hundreds of programs monthly on a range of topics, many of which are of interest to startups.
www.meetup.com

DEMO runs an annual tech conference for startups.
www.demo.com

TechCrunch Disrupt holds an annual conference.
http://techcrunch.com/event-type/disrupt

Startup Grind has numerous events both in Silicon Valley and around the world.
www.startupgrind.com

Resources

F6S has a weekly mailing that lists startup programs around the world
www.f6s.com

Bessemer Ventures provides information on the companies they passed on when investing.
www.bvp.com/portfolio/anti-portfolio/

PriceWaterhouseCoopers publishes a quarterly report on venture capital investment and trends.
www.pwcmoneytree.com

National Venture Capital Association provides model legal documents as well as an annual report on the venture capital industry.
http://nvca.org/resources/model-legal-documents
http://nvca.org/research/stats-studies

Re/code website includes much information of value to startups.
www.recode.net

Slideshare offers some helpful resources for startups, including presentations by investors and entrepreneurs that can be useful for gathering competitive information or for preparing one's own presentation.
www.slideshare.net

Leading law firm Orrick has a startup toolkit that features a term-sheet creator and standard legal forms.
https://orrick.com/Practices/Emerging-Companies/Pages/Startup-Tool-Kit.aspx

Garage Ventures provides a range of resources and information for startups.
http://www.garage.com/resources

CB Insights offers valuable information on venture capital investment news and trends. Sign up for the newsletter.
www.cbinsights.com

Link Silicon Valley provides helpful information on venture-backed companies, including their investors, management teams, and board members.
www.linksv.com

Venture Beat offers articles of interest and useful information on venture-backed companies.
www.venturebeat.com

Crunch Base has useful information on venture-backed companies.
www.crunchbase.com

Kickstarter is one of the key crowdfunding websites.
www.kickstarter.com

Indiegogo is another leading crowdfunding website.
www.indiegogo.com

AngelList is the website for finding angel investors.
https://angel.co

Books

Evans, Harold, and Gail Buckland. *They Made America*. New York: Back Bay Books, 2006.

> Provides background on many of the greatest inventions produced in the United States over the past 100-plus years.

Woodard, Colin. American Nations: *A History of the Eleven Rival Regional Cultures of North America*. New York: Viking, 2012.

> Provides a historical perspective on why there are differences in culture, values, and work styles in different parts of the United States.

Appendix B – The 10-Slide Presentation

Here is our recommended framework for a 10-slide presentation.

Cover Page   Company info: name, contact, email, and tagline

Problem   Customer profile and their problem—in *economic* terms

Solution   How and why it works, and the specific value to the customer

Market   Who the market is and how large it is

Distribution   How you will sell: channels, distribution, service, support

Business Model   How you will make money

Competition   Who else solves this problem, and how you and they compare

Team   Key personnel, relevant background, why this is the right team

Milestones   Financeable results that will be achieved, and when

Financials   How big, how fast, cash needed, and what the key assumptions are

Appendix C – G/Score Startup Benchmark and Assessment Methodology

Use this as a discussion framework during company assessments and pitch coaching

Overall Concept		**Is this a compelling, innovative solution that meets a clear and large market need?**
	4	An exciting concept that will appeal to a mass- or high-value market. Concept may be highly disruptive to existing players or enable significant new value creation for its customers.
	3	Concept addresses a clear market need or interest that currently is not well served by other solutions or competitors.
	2	Concept meets a market need in a differentiated manner; however, market is currently served by some viable alternatives.
	1	Concept doesn't meet a clear and/or significant market need. It is not clearly differentiated from alternatives currently addressing the market.
Market Opportunity		**How big is market size and/or business opportunity?**
	4	Substantial global market (>$1B potential) with no dominant competitor or alternative solution.
	3	Large global market ($1B potential) served by a range of alternative solutions or competitors, but where no single competitor has majority market share.
	2	Significant global or domestic market currently well served by alternative solutions or competitors where one or more competitors have a dominant market position.
	1	Small (>$500M) local or vertical market segment and/or market currently well served by one or more dominant players.
Competition & Business Risk		**How significant are the business and technical risks?**
	4	No dominant competitor, or comparable alternative approach, in the market and/or the solution is highly disruptive to current market leaders. Technical and implementation risks are well understood.
	3	Multiple competitors but no single market leader. Solution is well differentiated, market channels are well understood.
	2	Many strong competitors. Solution is not significantly differentiated. Competitive advantage may not be sustainable.
	1	Many dominate competitors. Technical and implementation challenges not well understood. No clear plan to enter and disrupt current market.
Product Execution		**Is product complete and demonstrating strong product/market fit?**
	4	Product complete and in the market with growing adoption by target customers.
	3	Product is in beta release with early customers. Promising feedback is driving further implementation.
	2	Product is pre-release (alpha). Concepts have been tested with target customers.
	1	Product is concept and/or first prototype only. No significant market testing has occurred.

		Are key business infrastructure and appropriate channel partners in place to support growth?
Business Execution	4	The business has established its go-to-market channels and partnerships. Key infrastructure is in place to reach and service customers, deliver product to market, support growth and expansion.
	3	The business is supported by established management and organizational practices and processes. IP protections, as necessary, are in place. Key partnerships have been established.
	2	Key business structures are in place. Founders have engaged appropriate advisors/board members to guide strategy. Go-to-market partnerships are in formation.
	1	The business is newly formed (may or may not be legally structured) using rudimentary tools to manage business operations. No significant channel and/or go-to-market partnerships have been established.
		Are an experienced executive team and appropriate personnel management practices in place?
Team	4	The management team is complete and key executives have relevant experience to execute on the market opportunity. Appropriate personnel management systems are in place.
	3	The management team is near-complete, but lacking one or more key executives with appropriate market and business experience for the current opportunity. Human Resource practices are not fully established.
	2	Founding management team is in place, but with critical gaps in the organizational structure (e.g., missing financial or marketing executive). Key roles filled by contractors rather than employees.
	1	Founder(s) only. May be lacking key business, market, or technical skills.
		Does the company understand the metrics of its business? Is the business model working?
Business Model & Customer	4	The business is operating on a clear, proven business model. Cost and pricing, customer acquisition model and metrics are well understood. Customers are buying. Business is meeting revenue and growth objectives.
	3	The business has developed a clear revenue and business model, established pricing and customer acquisition strategies. Early market tests demonstrate willingness to buy. Business has not hit growth objectives to date.
	2	The revenue and business model is defined, but concepts have not been widely tested.
	1	No clear path to revenue. No understanding of customer and/or channel requirements.

Looking for Entrepreneurs in the Most Unique Places

Great Wall, China

Near Tanis, Tunisia

Tiananmen Square, Beijing

Cairo Egypt

Zipaquirá, Colombia

Acknowledgments

We express our gratitude to all those who helped us through the process of writing this book. The people who reviewed early drafts of our manuscript gave us valuable feedback. They include Deborah Siegle, Carlos Pessoa Filho, Frank Bishop, Gloria Hunt, and Lene Sjorslev Schulze. A special note of appreciation goes to Susan Lucas-Conwell, who was gracious enough to read multiple drafts of the manuscript. In the first go-round, Susan gave us what we really needed—scathing comments and tough love. She pushed us to rewrite big chunks of the book, which resulted in a more focused manuscript with more substantive content.

We appreciate Holly Brady for her judicious editing assistance that helped bring clarity to the book and eliminated redundant, duplicative, and otherwise repetitive sections. And for reminding us to outline our ideas, something we both managed to conveniently forget a long time ago.

We want to thank Carsten, Heidi, Christian, William, Pernille and Camilla at Wibroe, Duckert and Partners in Copenhagen and in Silicon Valley, it is with an X (the lab) aka WDPX. This sharp team contributed creative inspiration, valuable expertise, and a detailed execution of the launch strategy and book cover design.

Thank you to Keith Milne, the book's interior designer, for fulfilling our vision of an easily accessible and readable book.

Thanks also to Ellie Baer, for taking some great photos of Silicon Valley icons.

To Maia Buzbee, sincere appreciation for the interior graphic in chapter 2.

To Ally Boville, for transcribing many, many interviews.

To Asa Mathat, for the author photographs and his supporting team of Skyler Stanley, Danielle Tolson & Chris Shipley.

To Elsie Atienza, for your wickedly wonderful sense of humor and tolerance for our comings and goings in the White Summers office. You are a real joy to be around.

To all our interviewees, for their time, perspectives, and wisdom. They fit us into their busy schedules and provided great insight.

- Derek Andersen, Startup Grind
- Selcuk Atli, Serial Entrepreneur
- Kayvan Baroumand, SV101 Ventures
- Rachel Faller, Tonlé Designs
- Balacz Farago, Real 5D
- Diane Flynn, GSVlabs
- Viki Forrest, ANZA Technology Network
- Bill Grosso, Scientific Revenue
- Joe Kennedy, Pandora
- Danilo Leao, BovControl
- David Lee, SK Telecom
- Phil Libin, Evernote & General Catalyst Partners
- Susan Lucas-Conwell, Innovation Catalyst
- Dave McClure, 500 Startups
- Peter Marcotullio, SRI International
- Beverly Parenti, The Last Mile
- Martin Pichinson, Agency iP
- Fabio Santini, Neteye
- Lene Sjorslev Schulze, 42 Associates
- John Scull, Southern Cross Venture Partners

- Chris Shipley, Tech Analyst

- Andy Tsao, Silicon Valley Bank

- Mark White, White Summers Caffee & James

- Ann Winblad, Hummer Winblad Venture Partners

- Chris Yeh, PBWorks

- Zia Yusuf, BCG

To Bob Karr, for having the audacity to introduce us to one another many years ago. We thank you for this.

To Mark Woodworth, we appreciate your copy editing expertise.

A special thank you to Mark White, for making his conference room available over the past year, and for his willingness to be a sounding board as we struggled with various topics in the book.

We would like to thank our family and friends. When we proposed writing this book, they did not say, *You're crazy.* Rather, they were encouraging and supportive as we stumbled through the fog.

Finally, we especially want to thank all the entrepreneurs we've met on our journey both in Silicon Valley and around the world. We particularly appreciate the entrepreneurs outside the Valley who continually make us aware of how much we take for granted in the Valley. Building success is hard everywhere, but in many ways it's harder outside Silicon Valley.

About the Authors

Michelle E. Messina

Michelle Messina is CEO of the international advisory and training firm Explora International. She is a serial entrepreneur who brings strong sales, marketing, and business development skills to startups everywhere. Michelle pioneered the Silicon Valley best practices training of startups in 2004 and has worked in more than 40 countries. She has worked with leading corporate, university, and government acceleration programs to train startups, investors and mentors globally. She is also a corporate board member who helps companies get clear and focused, so they can translate their vision into reality. Michelle believes that being an entrepreneur is the hardest thing you'll ever enjoy doing.

Michelle's LinkedIn profile is **www.linkedin.com/in/michellemessina** and can be reached at **mmessina@explorainternational.com**.

Jonathan C. Baer

Jon Baer is Managing Partner at StoneHearth Ventures (formerly named Threshold Ventures) and a recovering venture capitalist who loves working with companies around the world. He was a general partner at a Sand Hill Road venture fund and the founder and CEO of two venture backed companies. He now spends his time teaching, mentoring, and advising early-stage companies at leading accelerators and universities as well as serving on several boards. Jon is expert at training startups, mentors and early stage investors in the best practices of Silicon Valley. He believes that startups require tough love; and need to focus on money, metrics, and milestones. Jon teaches startup CEOs to say less, because less is more.

Jon's LinkedIn profile is **www.linkedin.com/in/jonbaersiliconvalley** and can be reached at **jbaer@stonehearthventures.com**.

To email both authors simultaneously: **authors@decodingsiliconvalley.com**.